Dangerous
Animals

Fog City Press
814 Montgomery Street
San Francisco, CA 94133 USA

ISBN 1 74089 359 X

Printed and bound in China

Color reproduction by Colourscan Co Pte Ltd

DISCOVERIES

Dangerous Animals

CONSULTING EDITORS

Dr John Seidensticker

Curator of Mammals, National Zoological Park
Smithsonian Institution, Washington D.C.

Dr Susan Lumpkin

Director of Communications, Friends of the National Zoo;
Editor of *ZooGoer* magazine, Washington D.C.

FOG CITY PRESS

Contents

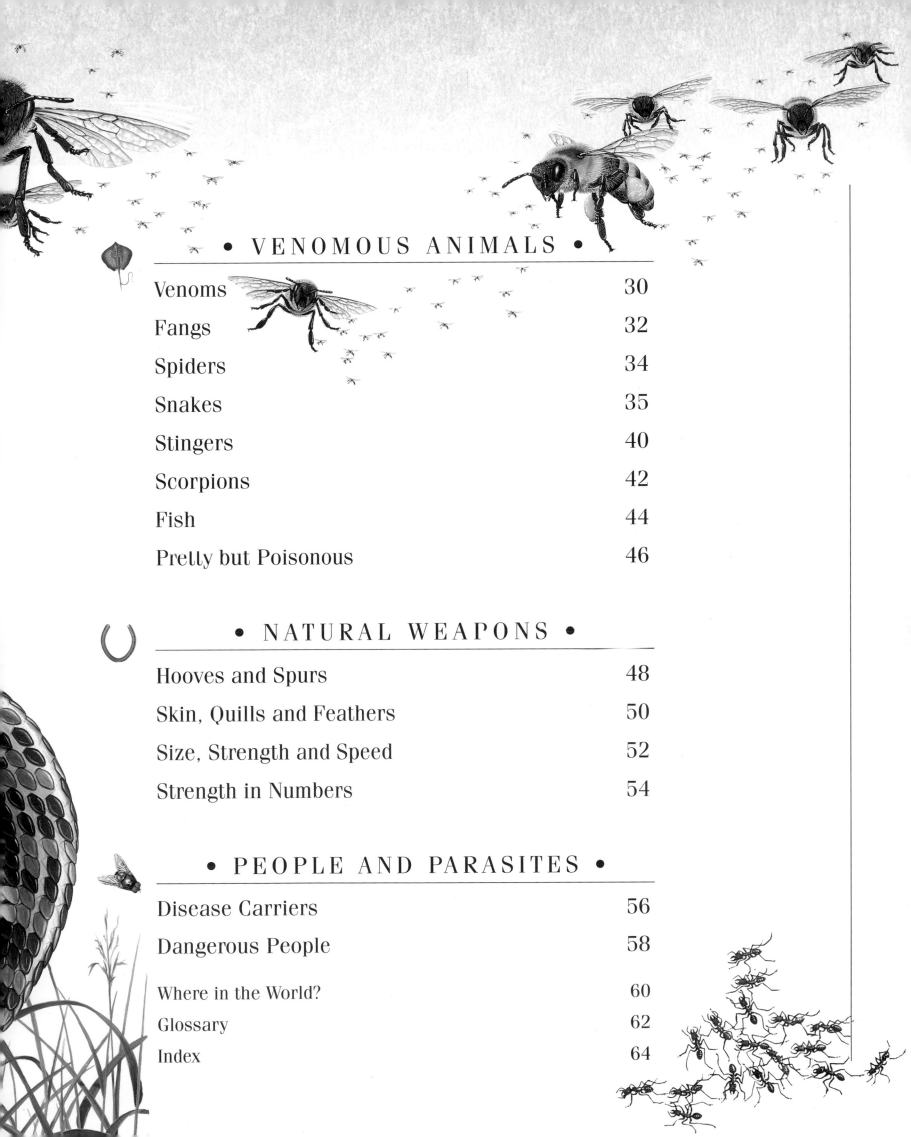

Death adder

Why Are Animals Dangerous?

The world is full of dangerous animals with powerful weapons for capturing prey and fighting off predators. A hunting tiger can kill with just one bite to the neck. A rhinoceros can spear a soft belly with its horn. Even a tiny spider can kill with venom-filled fangs. Animals' weapons are complex and varied. Teeth and claws, horns and hooves, fangs and stingers, spurs and spines, poisons and venoms, speed and stealth are all used to eat and avoid being eaten. Dangerous animals, such as snakes, seldom single out people as prey. People usually become victims when they scare or threaten an animal. Mosquitoes, ticks and flies, which cause disease and death, are very dangerous to people. But the most dangerous creatures of all are people.

TAIL STING
A scorpion's stinger injects predators or prey with powerful venom.

SEEING CLEARLY
Good eyesight helps predators such as lions and eagles to find prey. Other animals, such as sharks and bears, have poor vision. They can mistake people for their natural prey.

DID YOU KNOW?

Beware a black spider with red markings. This could be the female black widow, one of the most feared spiders in the world. A bite from this ferocious creature can cause dreadful pain, dizziness and death.

DEATH TRAPS
Birds of prey use powerful, sharp-edged beaks to kill their victims.

FATAL FUNNEL-WEB
A bite from the toxic fangs of Australia's funnel-web spider can be fatal, especially for children.

Barracuda

BULLDOG ANTS
Bulldog ants use their knife-edged biting jaws and venom-filled stingers to kill prey and scare off predators.

HORNS OF POWER
Plant-eating mammals, such as rhinoceroses and deer, use their horns and antlers to spear, stab and gore predators that threaten to make a meal of them. The males fight furiously with these weapons in battles over females.

A REAL MOUTHFUL
With up to 32 teeth in the upper jaw and 40 in the lower, a crocodile has the edge on most prey. Few animals can escape their fate if they are caught in a crocodile's teeth and jaws.

RIPPERS
A bear's claws can tear apart almost anything in its path.

7

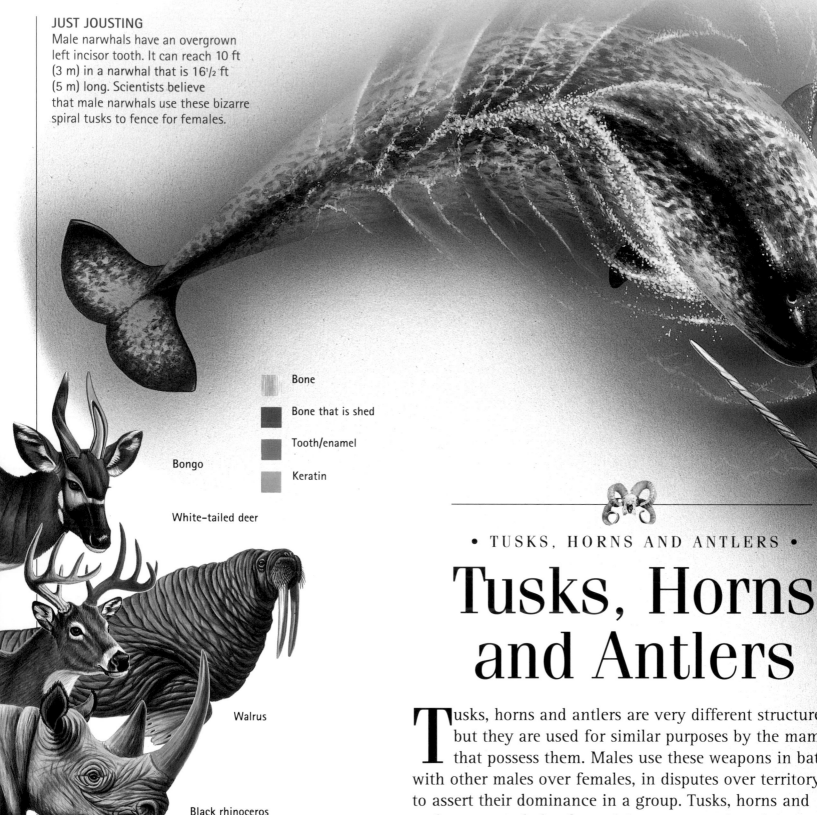

JUST JOUSTING

Male narwhals have an overgrown left incisor tooth. It can reach 10 ft (3 m) in a narwhal that is 16½ ft (5 m) long. Scientists believe that male narwhals use these bizarre spiral tusks to fence for females.

Bone

Bone that is shed

Tooth/enamel

Keratin

Bongo

White-tailed deer

Walrus

Black rhinoceros

SKIN AND BONE

Tusks, horns and antlers are made of different things. Walrus and elephant tusks are actually overgrown teeth. Bongo, cow and gazelle horns are bone, covered with hard skin called keratin. Rhinoceros horns are also made of keratin. Like all skin, they will grow back if worn down or cut off. The bone of deer, elk and moose antlers is covered with soft skin, called velvet, which falls off when the antlers reach full size. Horns are permanent, but antlers are temporary.

• TUSKS, HORNS AND ANTLERS •

Tusks, Horns and Antlers

Tusks, horns and antlers are very different structures, but they are used for similar purposes by the mammals that possess them. Males use these weapons in battles with other males over females, in disputes over territory or to assert their dominance in a group. Tusks, horns and antlers are symbols of a male's age, strength and status, and they can also help to prevent physical combat. A male with long tusks or elaborate antlers can beat a male with lesser weapons without exchanging a single blow; the weaker male knows it would be foolish to fight. In many species, only males grow tusks, horns and antlers. In others, females have smaller ones than males. But any male or female mammal with these weapons is potentially dangerous. If the animal uses them on a threatening predator, or a person, they can cause death.

CURIOUS CREATURE

The legend of the unicorn, a mystical creature with the body of a horse and a single, long horn on its head, probably came from exaggerated descriptions of rhinoceroses. In the past, people thought that unicorns had magical abilities. They believed that if they drank from a cup made of "unicorn" horn (probably acquired from a narwhal or a rhinoceros), they would be protected against poisoned liquids.

CLASHING ANTLERS

During the mating season, rival male moose have contests to find out which is the stronger. They will confront each other, nose to nose. If one does not retreat, they will bellow out challenges, then lock their antlers in a battle of strength and endurance. Straining every muscle to outpush each other, they will clash head-on. Usually the weaker one will turn away, but sometimes they will fight to the death. The winner mates with a moose cow and stays with her for several days.

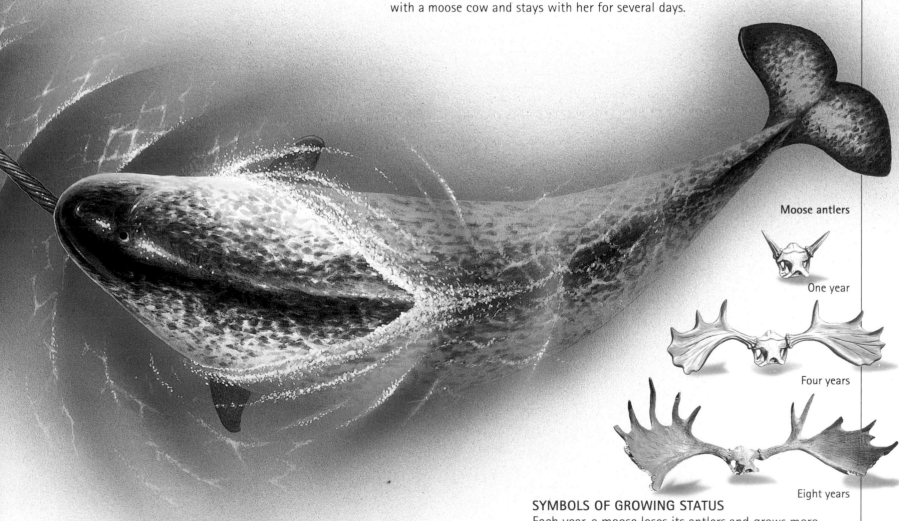

Moose antlers

One year

Four years

Eight years

SYMBOLS OF GROWING STATUS

Each year, a moose loses its antlers and grows more. The antlers become bigger and heavier as the moose gets older. Antlers are signs of a male's status and dominance in contests for food and females.

Elephants and Hippopotamuses

AFRICAN ELEPHANT
African elephants have very large ears, which they flap when they want to cool down. They often wallow in thick mud, which protects their skin from the sun and insects.

African and Asian elephants and the African hippo are three of the largest land animals. Imagine the combined weights of 90 ten-year-old children. This would equal the weight of one hippo. If you added another 100 children, this would be the weight of an African elephant. The huge size of these animals means that they eat enormous amounts of vegetation. Hippos live mostly in the water, but they feed on grass at night, clipping it with their thick lips to leave what looks like a mowed lawn. Elephants feed on grass, leaves and fruit, sometimes using their tusks to fell trees and uproot shrubs. Male elephants and hippos will fight and defend themselves with their tusks. Predators rarely take on adult elephants or hippos, but lions or tigers may threaten the babies of these animals. Female elephants and hippos will slash or stab menacing predators with their tusks.

ASIAN ELEPHANT
An Asian elephant is smaller than an African elephant, and its back, forehead, belly, teeth and trunk are a different shape.

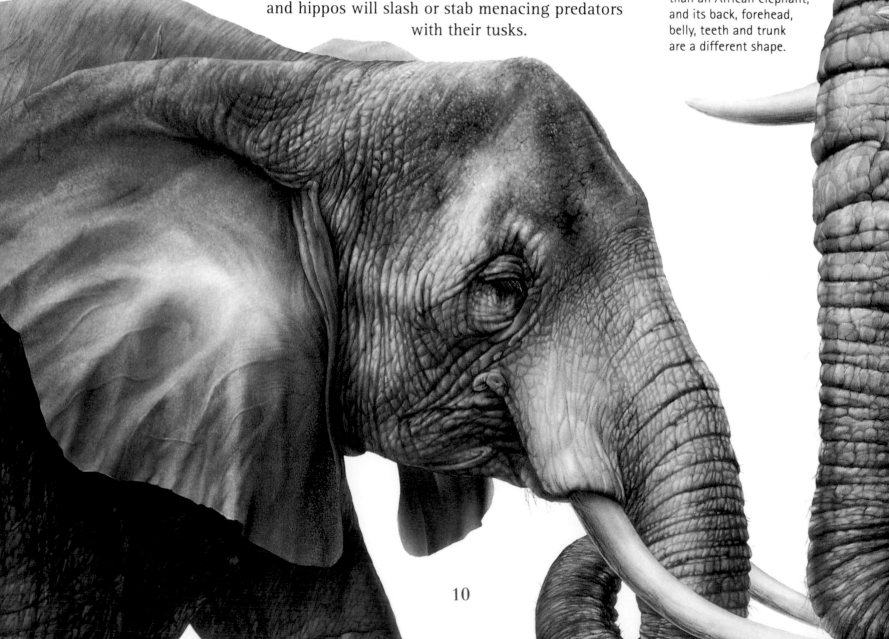

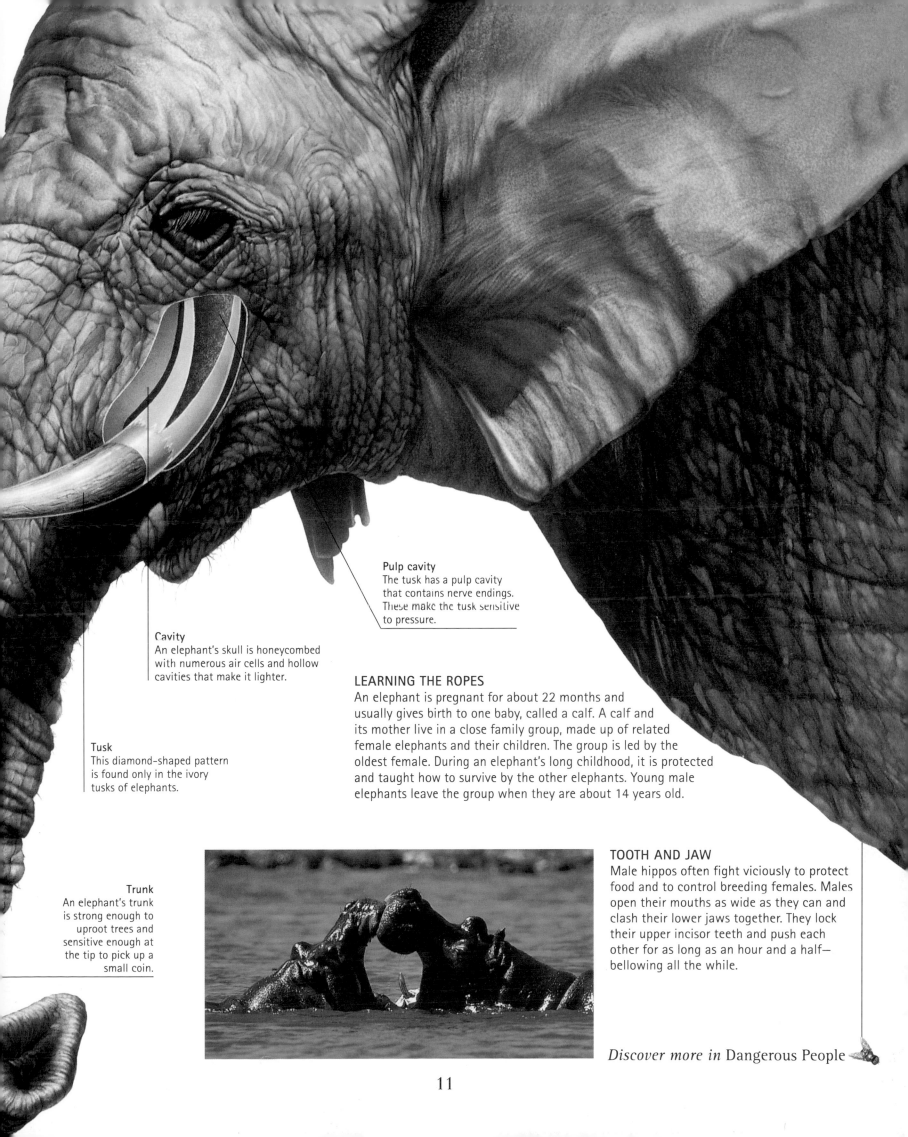

Pulp cavity
The tusk has a pulp cavity that contains nerve endings. These make the tusk sensitive to pressure.

Cavity
An elephant's skull is honeycombed with numerous air cells and hollow cavities that make it lighter.

Tusk
This diamond-shaped pattern is found only in the ivory tusks of elephants.

Trunk
An elephant's trunk is strong enough to uproot trees and sensitive enough at the tip to pick up a small coin.

LEARNING THE ROPES
An elephant is pregnant for about 22 months and usually gives birth to one baby, called a calf. A calf and its mother live in a close family group, made up of related female elephants and their children. The group is led by the oldest female. During an elephant's long childhood, it is protected and taught how to survive by the other elephants. Young male elephants leave the group when they are about 14 years old.

TOOTH AND JAW
Male hippos often fight viciously to protect food and to control breeding females. Males open their mouths as wide as they can and clash their lower jaws together. They lock their upper incisor teeth and push each other for as long as an hour and a half— bellowing all the while.

Discover more in Dangerous People

Rhinoceroses and Wild Cattle

Wild cattle, such as buffalo and bison, are related to domestic cows, and rhinos are related to horses. Unlike their relatives, however, rhinos and wild cattle are big and aggressive, and armed with formidable horns. There are five species of rhino: three live in tropical Asia and two in Africa. The several kinds of wild cattle can be found in Asia, Africa, North America and Europe. Wild cattle eat grass, while rhinos live on a mixed vegetarian diet of grass, leaves and fruit. Rhinos and wild cattle usually defend themselves by attacking. Faced with a predator– they charge. Competing males may also charge each other before sparring with their horns. These large mammals are more than a match for predators– except for well-armed people, who have greatly reduced the number of these animals wherever they are found.

ANCIENT ANIMAL ART
The earliest human art showed animals that our ancestors feared, admired or hunted. Wild cattle,are the subjects of many ancient paintings. This cave painting of a rhino and a bison was found in Lascaux, France, in an area of the cave called "Shaft of the Dead Man."

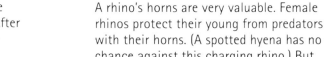

THE SIZE OF IT
Asian gaurs and wood bison are bigger than Sumatran rhinos. After elephants, white rhinos are the largest living mammals.

A HORNED DILEMMA
A rhino's horns are very valuable. Female rhinos protect their young from predators with their horns. (A spotted hyena has no chance against this charging rhino.) But rhinos are also killed by poachers for their horns. Scientists dehorned some female black rhinos to see if this would stop poachers from killing them. But the scientists found that without their horns, the rhinos could not defend their babies.

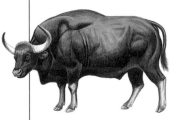

Gaur

Wood bison

White rhino

Sumatran rhino

DID YOU KNOW?

In Greek legends, the Minotaur was a half-man, half-bull monster, which lived in a maze that belonged to the King of Crete. Every year, the king sent 14 young men and women into the maze to be devoured by the bloodthirsty Minotaur. The Greek hero Theseus killed the ferocious creature.

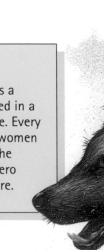

RAGING BULLS

The Spanish city of Pamplona is famed for its bull fights. Each year, the fiesta of San Fermin is celebrated with a "running of the bulls." Thousands of cheering residents and tourists watch people sprint through the city's narrow streets, chased by charging bulls.

Teeth, Jaws and Beaks

THE ONE THAT GOT AWAY
Taking a bite out of a surfboard is extremely easy for some sharks. The force of a bite from the short, protruding jaws of a whaler shark would be similar to dropping the weight of a truck onto the nail of your little finger.

Many dangerous vertebrates use teeth to catch, kill and eat prey. Teeth come in different shapes and sizes for different jobs. The razor-sharp teeth of a barracuda can tear hunks of flesh from fish. A crocodile's sharp, curved teeth both grasp and tear. Fish and crocodiles have just one kind of teeth, but mammals such as lions have several kinds. A lion's long canine teeth stab and hold like knives. Its scissor-like molars grip and rip chunks of flesh; incisors with serrated edges like a steak knife shear the last bits of meat from bones. Birds have no teeth at all. Instead, the beaks of some birds come in different shapes and sizes to spear, grip, bite, crush or tear flesh from prey. The power of teeth or beaks depends on the shape and size of an animal's jaws, and how the muscles attach the lower jaw to the rest of the skull.

DID YOU KNOW?

The crocodile has been feared and worshipped for centuries. The ancient Egyptians believed that the crocodile was Sebek, the god of the Nile. Children often wore necklaces of crocodile teeth to protect them from harm.

CONSPICUOUS CANINES

The sabertooth cat, which is now extinct, had extraordinary teeth. The sabertooth's skull was about the same size as that of a lion, but its impressive canines were more than twice as long as a lion's teeth. However, these long curved teeth with sharp serrated edges were not very strong and broke easily. Lions use their canines to crush neck bones or strangle prey. Sabertooth cats stabbed their prey's soft fleshy areas, such as the abdomen, with their unusual canines, before tearing out the inner organs.

SLIP, SLIDING AWAY
Mergansers are a type of duck. They are sometimes called sawbills because they have unusual long, thin beaks with sharp jagged edges. Mergansers capture and hold onto small slippery fish with their sawlike "teeth." Then they swallow the fish whole, rather than chewing it.

A MIXED DIET

A bear has relatively short canines, which it uses to catch and kill prey. Its flattened upper and lower molars, however, show that the bear is not a strict meat eater. It uses its grinding molars to shred and break down the plants, nuts and berries that form a large part of its diet.

CUTTING TEETH

A crocodile can puncture, grip and crush prey with its many teeth, but it cannot chew with them. Crocodile teeth do not have strong roots and they come out easily with wear. Luckily, for the crocodile anyway, it continually replaces old teeth with new.

HIGH-SPEED CHASE

Barracudas use rapid charges and daggerlike teeth to capture all kinds of fish. Sometimes they herd schools of fish to make them easier to catch. The largest of the barracudas lives in the western Atlantic and can grow to be as long as an adult man.

A NUTRITIOUS MEAL
A grizzly bear uses its sharp claws and teeth to eat a tasty meal of salmon from the river.

FLYING FISHER
An osprey is the envy of any fisher: it can catch a fish in nine out of every ten attempts. A hunting osprey flies in a figure eight, high above the water. When it spies a fish, such as a mullet, it plunges feet first to grab the fish out of the water. Spiny growths on the back of its strong toes help the osprey keep its grip on the slippery fish while it carries the prey off to a perch to be eaten.

• TEETH AND CLAWS •

Feet, Claws and Talons

D angerous animals use their claws, talons and feet to capture prey. Claws and talons are stronger, sharper versions of the nails that protect the tips of your fingers and toes. Some mammals, such as jaguars, use long, sharp claws to grab and hold prey before killing it with their teeth. Polar bears seize seals in their clawed forefeet, while grizzly bears snare salmon with theirs. Sturdy claws are also useful for climbing trees, digging up roots and slashing a predator or rival. Some birds rely on their feet and talons to get food. Osprey plunge from the sky, grabbing a fish with their strong feet and piercing it with their talons. Peregrine falcons swat birds with their powerful feet, then catch the stunned creatures in mid-air.

SWITCHBLADES

C ats depend on claws to catch their prey. A claw works like a switchblade. The blade's usual position is folded into a knifecase, but it springs out with a flick of a wrist. In the same way, a cat's claws usually remain retracted (pulled in), protected in sheaths of skin. They emerge from their sheaths only when the cat needs them.

CLAWS IN
In the retracted, or usual, state the elastic spring ligament is contracted and the controlling muscles are relaxed.

CLAWS OUT
When the muscles contract, the ligament stretches and the claw springs out, ready for action.

DID YOU KNOW?

The powerful owl hunts prey at night. Sometimes it holds any remains of the prey in its talons all day, and finishes it off as a snack before the night's hunt.

Sea eagle

Brown goshawk

Sparrowhawk

FINELY TUNED TALONS

A raptor's talons and toes match its prey. Sea eagles have long, sharply curved talons and sturdy toes, which help them to capture large, slippery fish in one foot. A brown goshawk's talons and toes grab squirrel-sized prey. The sparrowhawk's slender toes and needle-sharp talons are designed to snare small birds.

Discover more in Birds of Prey

17

Great Cats

All cats are good hunters. They have razor-sharp teeth, strong jaws, piercing claws and supple bodies. But only lions, tigers, jaguars, leopards, pumas, snow leopards and cheetahs can be called "great cats." These large, powerful beasts prey on animals such as deer and antelope. Occasionally, great cats, such as tigers, lions and leopards, will prey deliberately on humans. Only cheetahs and snow leopards have never reportedly killed humans, although both could easily do so. It is, however, more usual for a great cat to attack people when it is too sick, old, or maimed to capture its normal prey, or when this prey is scarce. We may fear great cats, but they have much to fear from us. Some people hunt them illegally for their skins, while others turn their wild habitats into farms and logged forests. All seven species of great cats are endangered.

FAST FOOD

A lioness slowly and silently approaches a Thompson's gazelle. With an incredible burst of speed, she closes the gap between herself and the gazelle, grabs the frightened animal in her paws and kills it with a piercing bite to the neck. Other lionesses and lions will soon join her in devouring the carcass.

IN FOR THE KILL

Most great cats kill their prey by biting into the back of the neck with their canine teeth to cut the prey's spinal cord. But to kill very large animals, such as buffalo, lions and other great cats squeeze the prey by the throat until it suffocates. The lion's large paws and sharp claws help drag the animal to the ground.

SPOTTED SPEED

Cheetahs outclass all other land animals for short-distance sprinting. A spring-like spine coils and uncoils to help them speed along at 70 miles (110 km) per hour. The cheetah's long, streaming tail acts as a steering rudder.

DID YOU KNOW?

In the past, many people thought that eating the meat of a lion would give them courage. In paintings and books, the lion often stands for power and strength. The Cowardly Lion in the story *The Wizard of Oz* believes he has no courage. He asks the Wizard of the Emerald City to make him brave.

GUARANTEEING THE FUTURE

Big-game hunters killed thousands of tigers for "sport" until laws passed in the 1970s banned tiger hunting for profit or sport. But the 5,000 or so tigers left in the wild are still hunted and poached illegally. Unless this stops, tigers may become extinct in the next 20 years.

A RARE SIGHT
Pumas are large and strong, but very shy. They live and hunt alone, and capture all kinds of prey— from deer and elk to ground squirrels, mice and even grasshoppers, if big game is scarce. Pumas avoid people and very rarely attack them.

Discover more in Size, Strength and Speed

Wolves and Wild Dogs

Wolves travel widely to find prey such as deer and moose. When they sight a victim, they slowly sneak up on it, until, sensing danger, the prey flees. The wolves then rush to attack. Using 42 deadly teeth in their powerful jaws, some wolves bite the prey's rump to slow it down. One wolf, usually the pack leader, darts forward to seize its nose. Others nip and rip its flanks, neck and throat. Within minutes, the prey has been bitten to death and the wolves are tearing into their dinner. Although the wolves cooperate to make the kill, it is every wolf for itself when it comes to eating it. Many of the 35 species of wolves and their wild dog relatives live in groups and hunt large prey together. These groups may number 20 wild dogs, able to take down a zebra, or be as small as a pair of foxes, which often hunt for small prey, such as rabbits and rodents.

THE HUNTER AND THE HUNTED
A maned wolf roams the grassy pampas of Brazil. These long-legged animals can cover long distances, hunting rodents, rabbits and birds. Some people believe that parts of the maned wolf's body, such as the eye, are lucky. As a result, many have been killed, and they are now an endangered species.

TALKING TAILS

If a dog is afraid, it will walk with its tail between its legs. In the same way, a wolf uses its tail to tell other wolves about its moods and intentions.

NO PROBLEM
This is the tail of a relaxed wolf or dog. Wolves that are eating or just looking around casually will hold their tails loosely, and their fur will be slightly fluffed.

NO THREAT
A wolf holding its tail close to its body, with the tip curved back and the fur flattened, is saying, "I'm no threat." It may be approaching a dominant wolf, perhaps to beg for food.

FEARFUL
When a wolf is afraid, its tail touches its belly. A wolf holds its tail like this when it loses a serious fight with a dominant wolf.

BACK OFF
With its tail held high and the fur fluffed out to make it look bigger, this wolf is saying, "I can beat you, so you had better back off."

ATTACK
If you see a wolf or an unfriendly dog holding its tail straight out behind it, think about how to escape— quickly! This animal plans to attack.

HOWL AWAY
At close range, wolves communicate with whimpers, growls, barks and squeaks. But howling can capture the attention of wolves far and wide. When all pack members join in an echoing chorus, they can be heard as far as 6 miles (10 km) away. Group howling sends a message to neighboring packs: stay away, or come prepared to fight. Wolves also howl to locate pack members that have lost one another during a long chase after prey. Once reunited, they howl in celebration.

Bears

What do you picture when you think of a bear? A giant panda, a fierce grizzly bear or maybe the honey-loving, storybook character, Winnie the Pooh? It probably depends on where you live. One or more of the eight species of bear lives among people in the ice of the Arctic; the temperate forests in Europe, Asia and North America; and tropical forests in Asia and South America. Bears are enormous creatures with heavy bodies, long, sharp claws and huge heads with long canine teeth. Polar bears use these weapons to kill seals, but other bears use them to dig up roots, strip bark, split bamboo and rip open beehives. These bears eat plants, insects, honey and meat, if they can catch it easily. Giant pandas live on bamboo, spectacled bears prefer fruits and nuts, and sloth bears eat termites. Bears use their teeth and claws to fight each other, to defend their young and sometimes to attack people who get in the way.

DOWN AND OUT

Using its keen sense of smell, a grizzly bear finds a marmot's underground home. It rips off the roof of the marmot's burrow with its claws and scoops out the exposed animal.

A BIRD'S EYE VIEW
A cinnamon-colored black bear snoozes in a treetop. When there are people around, black bears often sleep in places where it would be difficult for someone to creep up on them.

A TALE OF TWO FISHERS
Fishermen and grizzly bears are both attracted by abundant salmon. The catch can be shared peacefully if people follow the rules: do not get close and do not act in any surprising manner. Grizzly attacks usually occur when people startle a mother protecting her cubs, or when they "invite" the bears to dinner by keeping food in their camping tents.

DID YOU KNOW?
The teddy bear is named after Theodore "Ted" Roosevelt, the 26th President of the United States. He refused to shoot a black bear while on a hunting trip.

UP AND AWAY
American black bears are excellent tree climbers. They climb quickly, using their short, sturdy claws to keep a firm grip on the tree. When in danger, bear cubs scramble into the tree tops while their mother fights or flees alone. Later, she returns to fetch them. American black bears also climb into trees to reach food, such as honey from beehives.

WHITE KNIGHTS
Huge male polar bears fight viciously with their large, sharp claws and canine teeth when they compete for females during the breeding season. The loser of the battle is often killed.

• TEETH AND CLAWS •

Birds of Prey

If you see a bird with a hooked beak, big staring eyes and strong feet with sharp talons, you are looking at a bird of prey. These raptors live throughout the world, except in Antarctica. Size, diet and hunting style vary greatly among the 463 species. Robin-sized falconets catch flying insects. Crow-sized sparrowhawks snatch smaller birds off the branches of trees. Secretary birds the size of turkeys hunt for small mammals and snakes on the ground. Condors with wingspans as wide as the smallest airplane eat the meat of dead animals. South America's harpy eagle is one of the largest raptors. It can seize and carry off a monkey the size of a big house cat. Most raptors, such as falcons, hunt during the day, although owls hunt at night. Many birds of prey are strong and spectacular flyers. Golden eagles cover huge distances looking for food and swoop from great heights to attack unsuspecting prey on the ground.

IN HOT PURSUIT
Reaching flight speeds of 80 miles (128 km) per hour, this peregrine falcon will quickly overtake its pigeon prey. If it dives from high to capture a bird below, it can reach speeds of up to 178 miles (288 km) per hour!

NOWHERE TO RUN, NOWHERE TO HIDE
Huge harpy eagles hunt among the trees of the Amazon rainforest. Moving from tree to tree, they listen for the chatter of monkeys, and home in on their prey. A surprised howler monkey is no match for a harpy, which will snatch it up with feet as large as a man's hand.

READING THE MENU

Once or twice a day, most raptors regurgitate parts of their prey that they cannot digest. Scientists search avidly for these pellets, which reveal what a raptor has been eating. Fur in a pellet means mammals were on the raptor's menu, while feathers indicate birds, and scales say snakes. Often, scientists can pinpoint exactly which species of mammal, bird or snake the raptor ate, and how many were included on the menu!

Bones

Claws

Bird pellet

Crocodiles and Alligators

Resembling a log lying in the murky, shallow water, a crocodile will wait for an antelope to come for a drink. Only its eyes, ears and nose are out of the water, so it can see, hear and smell a thirsty animal nearing the shore. In a sudden lunge, the crocodile will vault out of the water and seize an antelope's muzzle in its clamping and gripping teeth. The crocodile will then flip or drag the antelope underwater and drown it. Stealth, speed and a snout full of sharp teeth are the weapons of the 22 species of crocodiles, alligators, caimans and gharial that live in tropical and subtropical lakes, rivers and sea coasts. These reptiles range from the length of a bike to as long as a limousine, but all are fierce meat eaters. They prey on any creature they can catch, from small fish to mammals as big as buffalo—and people of all sizes.

TELLING TEETH
Is it an alligator or a crocodile? You can tell the difference by looking at its teeth, but from a distance! Luckily, you do not have to peer too closely to see that an alligator's lower teeth cannot be seen when its mouth is closed. Its lower teeth fit into pits in the upper jaw. In a closed-mouthed crocodile, however, one lower tooth on each side slips into a notch on the outside of the upper jaw.

Alligator
Lower teeth hidden

Crocodile
Lower teeth showing

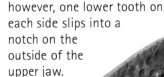
Alligator

DID YOU KNOW?
Female crocodiles and alligators bury their leathery eggs on land, then guard the nest constantly for 70 to 90 days. When they hear their babies crying, they uncover the eggs and crack the shells gently to help free them.

A WILDEBEEST WORTH PURSUING
A huge Nile crocodile chases a wildebeest. It will provide the crocodile with more meat than it can eat in one meal.

26

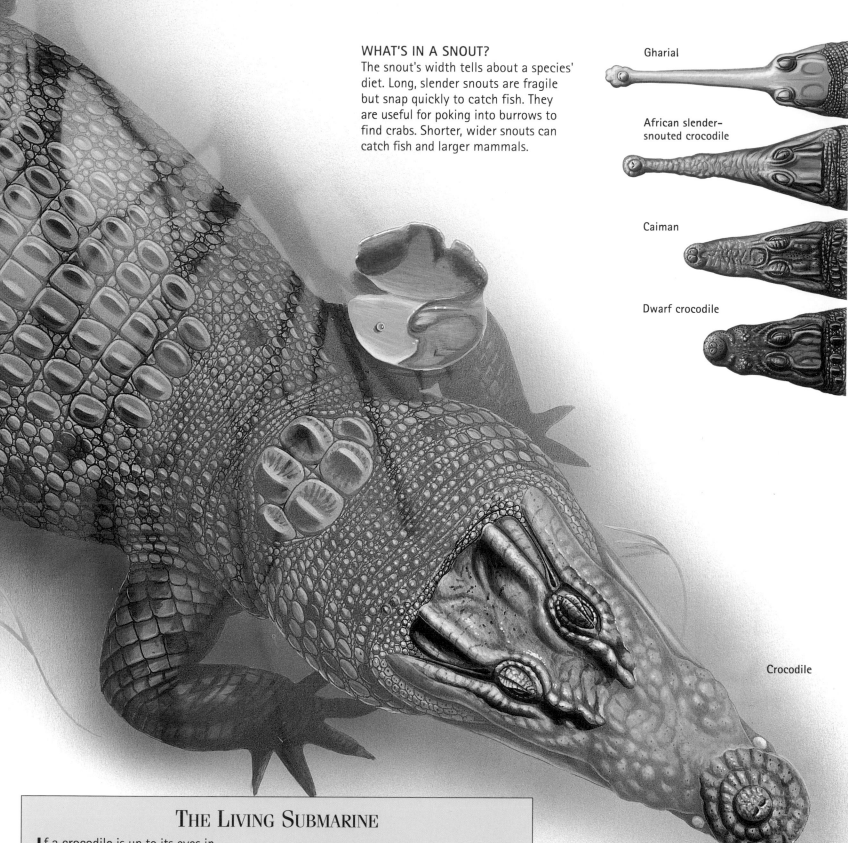

WHAT'S IN A SNOUT?

The snout's width tells about a species' diet. Long, slender snouts are fragile but snap quickly to catch fish. They are useful for poking into burrows to find crabs. Shorter, wider snouts can catch fish and larger mammals.

Gharial

African slender-snouted crocodile

Caiman

Dwarf crocodile

Crocodile

THE LIVING SUBMARINE

If a crocodile is up to its eyes in water and has a mouth full of food, how does it breathe? By using its nostrils, which are on the tip of its snout and out of the water. When the crocodile inhales, air flows through the nasal passage, and the smell chamber, to the windpipe. A throat valve, formed when a flap of skin at the back of the mouth meets one on the tongue, keeps water from entering the windpipe.

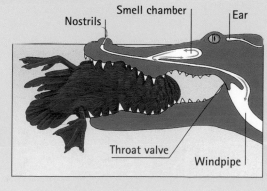

Nostrils

Smell chamber

Ear

Throat valve

Windpipe

ENERGY SAVERS

Crocodiles and alligators are lazy predators. They lie still, mostly submerged in shallow water, and wait for food to come to them. This energy-saving behavior and efficient digestion helps these animals to survive for months without a meal.

Discover more in Size, Strength and Speed

GREAT WHITE KILLER

The great white shark is the famous killer shark of the film *Jaws* and horror stories. Although its evil reputation is exaggerated, the great white shark may be the most dangerous predator of all to humans. Great whites prey mostly on seals and porpoises, but they do encounter people swimming in their hunting grounds. With their poor vision, they may see little difference between the size and sleek lines of a seal and a snorkeler.

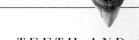

• TEETH AND CLAWS •

Sharks

Imagine splashing in the surf and suddenly seeing a grey fin slicing through the water towards you. One word comes to mind. Shark! With strong, slender bodies, sharks swim fast and lunge at prey even faster. They attack with a strong mouthful of sharp teeth, which they use to tear off chunks of their victim's flesh. The 350 species of sharks live in oceans throughout the world, from cold polar waters to tropical seas. But you are more likely to drown than see a shark, much less be attacked by one. Many sharks are small and eat fish, shellfish and clams. The biggest types, whale and basking sharks, eat tiny plants and animals called plankton. The most dangerous sharks, such as great whites and tiger sharks, hunt in shallow coastal waters. They may sometimes confuse human swimmers and divers with seals and porpoises, their natural prey.

Tiger shark
20 ft (6 m)

Blue shark
13 ft (4 m)

Bronze whaler shark
6½ ft (2 m)

Diver
6 ft (1.8 m)

THE SIZE ADVANTAGE

Most dangerous sharks are bigger than people. This means that sharks see people as prey they can attack without much risk to themselves. Big sharks are much faster than people in the water— and far better armed.

Sense organs

Pores

Electric sensory perception
Small pores on a shark's snout link to sense organs. They detect weak electrical impulses produced by prey and by the Earth's magnetic field. Sharks use this sense to find prey. It may also act as a compass to help guide sharks when they migrate.

USING SHARKS

To the Chinese gourmet, few dishes are as appealing, or as expensive, as shark-fin soup. In many other countries, shark meat appears regularly on restaurant menus and kitchen tables. People use sharks for leather, fertilizer, oils of various kinds and Vitamin A. Their eyes provide corneas for human eye transplants and shark cartilage is used for treating burns.

OPEN WIDE
Whale sharks, which grow up to 46 ft (14 m), are the world's largest fish. They eat plankton and small fish and use a grill in their mouths to trap and filter food.

Q : Are whale sharks or basking sharks likely to attack people?

Venoms

Many animals produce venoms or poisons to deter predators and capture prey. A spitting cobra can spray a stream of venom into the eyes of an enemy 10 ft (3 m) away. Blind and in terrible pain, the enemy, or an unsuspecting walker, drops to the ground and the snake slithers away. Animal venoms and poisons are complex combinations of chemicals that, drop for drop, are among the most toxic substances known. A dart-poison frog the size of a walnut contains enough poison to kill 100 people. The venom from a box jellyfish can kill someone in less time than it takes to read this page. A tiny fraction of a drop of Indian cobra venom can be fatal to a human. Venomous animals have special structures, such as fangs, spines or stingers, to inject poisons directly into the bodies of their predators or prey. But poisonous animals, such as dart-poison frogs, will kill you only if touched or eaten.

VENOM VARIETIES

AUSTRALIAN PARALYSIS TICK
The females feed on the blood of people and dogs. The saliva of a single feeding female may paralyze and even kill its host unless the tick is removed.

BLACK-HEADED SEA SNAKE
The most poisonous of all snakes, its venom is 100 times more toxic than that of the deadly taipan. It may cause paralysis and death within hours.

BLUE-RINGED OCTOPUS
This creature spits venomous saliva into its bite wound. Death may follow in minutes when the breathing muscles become paralyzed.

STONEFISH
The venomous spines of this fish produce violent pain, which spreads from the foot to the abdomen. Swelling, numbness, blisters, delirium and even death may follow.

NORTHERN AFRICAN SCORPION
This is the most deadly of all scorpions. Its venom attacks the nervous system, and adults may die within minutes of a sting.

FUNNEL-WEB SPIDER
Until antivenin was available, children were especially likely to die from this spider's bite. Males of this species are far more venomous than females.

BOX JELLYFISH
The venom from this jellyfish may lead to death from paralysis within 30 seconds to 15 minutes. Even a mild sting is very painful and leaves long-lasting scars.

POISONOUS PLATYPUS
A male platypus can paralyze a person's leg or kill a dog by wrapping his legs around the victim and jabbing it with venom-filled ankle spurs. These hollow spurs connect to venom glands, which produce more venom during the breeding season than at other times. Males wound and sometimes kill each other with their venomous spurs.

STRANGE BUT TRUE
Some shrews, such as this Eurasian water shrew, are the only mammals with venomous saliva. Shrews are not dangerous to people, but the salivary glands of one American short-tailed shrew have enough venom to kill 200 mice.

LIFE-SAVING LIQUID
Antivenins reverse or relieve the symptoms of some venomous bites and stings. They are available for most dangerous snakes, as well as some scorpions, ants, spiders and bees.

CAUTION
Funnel – Web
Spider Antivenom
100 mg (approx) of
Immune Rabbit IgG
125 units

SPITTING COBRA

In most snakes, venom pours out of the open tip of their hollow fangs, like water through a hose nozzle. But in the three species of spitting cobra, the venom sprays in a jet out of the opening, like water spraying from a puncture in a hose. These cobras only spit in defense; while hunting, they bite in typical snake fashion.

Fangs

Spiders and venomous snakes have fangs that deliver venom into prey or predators. The fangs of snakes are very long, slender teeth with grooves or hollow centers through which the venom flows. Pit vipers, rattlesnakes, cobras, coral snakes and others have fangs at the front of their mouths. These fangs are like hypodermic needles and inject venom into the prey's bloodstream. The deadly African boomslang and other snakes have fangs at the rear of their mouths. These snakes catch prey in their mouths and push it to the back of their jaws. As they chew it with their fangs, venom flows into the bitten areas. When the venom takes effect and the prey stops struggling, the snake swallows it. The sharp, thin fangs of spiders, which pierce, hold and tear prey, are the end parts of their paired jaws, or chelicerae. When muscles in the spiders' venom glands contract, venom is injected through the chelicerae. The fangs of a funnel-web spider are particularly intimidating. Like a pair of pickaxes, they are poised, ready to strike any unsuspecting insect.

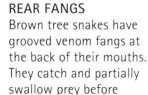

REAR FANGS
Brown tree snakes have grooved venom fangs at the back of their mouths. They catch and partially swallow prey before using their fangs.

DID YOU KNOW?
Venom can be more dangerous to some prey than to others. The eastern diamondback rattlesnake commonly eats rabbits, and its venom kills them very quickly. But this snake must inject more venom to kill an animal that is not usually on its menu.

STABBING FANGS
The fangs of rattlesnakes, such as this red diamondback, point forward to stab venom into their prey. While the fast-acting venom takes effect, the snake tracks down and eats its dead or dying meal.

BITE AND SQUEEZE
The eastern brown snake of Australia kills prey by injecting venom with its long fangs, or constricting with its coils. It will also strike to defend itself and can inject enough venom to kill a human.

FATAL FANGS
The needle-sharp fangs of a red-back spider puncture and hold its prey while the paralyzing venom begins to work.

Venom gland

VENOM SACS
The funnel-web's venom is stored in a pair of glands, or sacs, at the base of the fangs. When the spider bites, venom flows from the glands through ducts that end in small holes at the tips of the fangs.

FOLD-AWAY FANGS
Vipers and pit vipers, categories which include adders and rattlesnakes, have the most efficient fangs of all the venomous snakes. When not in use, these very large fangs fold neatly away in the roof of the snake's mouth and are covered by a flap of skin. But when the snake opens its mouth, the flap is pulled back and the fang springs forward and strikes. Pressure on the storage area forces venom down a duct to the fang and into the snake's victim.

Mouth closed; fangs back

Mouth open; fangs forward

FUNNEL-WEB FANGS
Australia's deadly funnel-web spider has two sharp fangs at the front of its head, or cephalothorax. This spider raises its head to attack and stabs its prey by moving its head down, with the fangs pointed downward. In many other kinds of spiders, the fangs are rotated to face each other. They move from side to side in a pinching action.

OPEN WIDE!
This halloween snake grabs a frog quickly and pulls the startled creature towards the fangs at the back of its mouth. Once the frog is injected with venom, it is unable to struggle and begins its journey down into the snake's stomach.

WIDER STILL!
Snakes usually swallow prey headfirst. Frogs, however, puff themselves up with air to make it difficult for an attacker to swallow them. Undaunted, snakes swallow frogs feet first, and squeeze the air back out through the frogs' mouths.

Elastic connection

Windpipe

Lower jaw

ELASTIC JAWS
Snakes have elastic connections between the bones in their lower jaw so that they can open their mouths very wide. They can extend the opening of their windpipes and continue to breathe while they swallow prey.

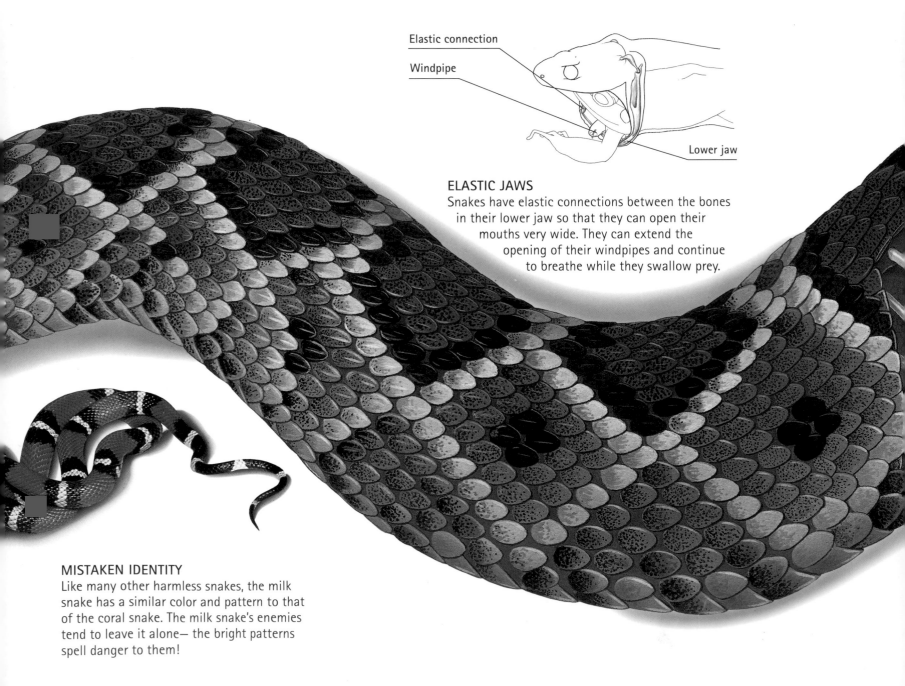

MISTAKEN IDENTITY
Like many other harmless snakes, the milk snake has a similar color and pattern to that of the coral snake. The milk snake's enemies tend to leave it alone— the bright patterns spell danger to them!

Snakes

HANDLE WITH CARE
Poisonous snakes are sometimes "milked" for their venom. The venom is used to make medicine called antivenin, which is an antidote for snakebite.

Snakes have a terrible reputation. Their slithering bodies fill people with revulsion and fear. But most snakes are not dangerous to people. Of the 2,700 species of snake in the world, only about 300 are venomous, and these usually strike only when they are threatened. Snakes cannot tear or bite pieces of flesh from their prey. Instead, they must swallow it whole. They have expandable, "elastic" jaws, which make it possible for them to open their mouths extremely wide. A large snake can swallow a pig or an antelope! Some snakes, such as brown tree snakes, rattlesnakes and cobras, use venom to subdue or kill large prey so that they can swallow it without a struggle. Constrictors, such as boas and pythons, wrap their bodies tightly around prey to suffocate it. Snakes without venom or constricting coils catch and swallow small, squirming prey.

Eyes
A snake's eyes are covered by a clear, transparent scale, which evolved from its lower eyelid. The scale is fixed in place and gives the snake an unblinking stare.

Venom gland
This gland stores the cloudy liquid venom. Venom passes through the venom ducts and into the hollow fangs.

Heat-sensitive pit
This pit senses even the smallest of temperature changes. A snake can tell exactly where prey is, even In the dark, by comparing the input from the right and left pits.

Fangs
Long fangs are hinged so they can be folded back into the mouth. When the snake opens its mouth, the fangs spring out, ready for action.

Forked tongue
The snake's forked tongue "tastes" the air and passes information about smell back to the snake's brain.

WARNING COLORS
This beautifully patterned coral snake is extremely poisonous. Its red, black and yellow bands warn its enemies to keep well away, or suffer a deadly bite.

Spiders

It is hard to avoid spiders. There are more than 30,000 different kinds of spiders, and they live all over the world. Some of these eight-legged invertebrates are almost too small to see, but others are as big as your fist. Spiders are dangerous predators of insects and other spiders. About half of all spiders capture prey in webs of silk, which vary from simple trip wires to complex, and sometimes huge, orbs. Other spiders either chase or ambush their victims. Spiders use venom from their fangs to kill or paralyze their prey, and to fight and defend themselves. Spiders bite people only in self-defense, and fewer than 30 kinds of spiders have venom that is poisonous to people. Many creatures, including people, are dangerous to spiders. Mammals, birds, reptiles, amphibians, other spiders and insects all prey on spiders.

TRICKY TRAPDOORS
Trapdoor spiders rarely leave their silk-lined underground burrows, which have silk doors. At night, they pounce on passing prey, bite it with their fangs, then eat it inside the burrow.

Hind legs
A spider uses its hind legs to turn prey while wrapping it in silk from its spinnerets.

Claws
A spider's jointed walking legs are tipped with claws. The claws allow the spider to grip the smooth silk of its web.

Spinnerets
Silk for spinning webs comes from the silk gland through tiny spinning tubes at the tips of these organs.

SCAFFOLD WEBS
The black widow spider builds a scaffold web to capture insects. Sticky silk lines, which stretch tightly from the web to the ground, catch a passing insect. As the insect struggles to get free, the line breaks from the ground and leaves it dangling in the air. The spider tows the stunned insect into the scaffold, ties it up with silk and delivers the killing bite.

Abdomen
This houses the digestive gland, the heart, the lungs, the reproductive organs and the silk glands.

STUCK TO IT

A redbacked orb-web spider waits for an insect to get caught in the sticky silk of its web. The trapped insect vibrates the web, which tells the spider a victim has arrived. The spider vibrates the web to further ensnare the prey, then kills it. The spider either eats its catch then, or wraps it in silk for later.

Cephalothorax
In spiders, the head and thorax are joined and contain the eyes, mouth, poison gland, stomach and "brain." The underside is called the sternum.

Palps
These jointed limbs are the sense organs. In males, the tips are enlarged and are used to transfer sperm to a female during mating.

Fangs
These are on the tip of the spider's first limb (called a chelicera).

Pedicel
This is the narrow waist that joins the spider's abdomen and cephalothorax.

FISHING SPIDER

Perched on a floating leaf, a fishing spider dangles its front legs in the water. When a fish gets close, the spider attacks. The fish succumbs quickly to the spider's gripping bite and strong venom. The spider then drags the fish back to its leaf and enjoys its dinner.

THE WEB IT WEAVES

An orb-weaving spider waits for a breeze to blow a silken thread from one stem to another. The spider adds more silk to make it strong and tight, and spins a loosely attached line. The spider sits in the center of this line and pulls it into a V shape, then spins another line straight down to form a Y shape. Working from the base of the V, or hub, the spider attaches lines until the web looks like a sliced pie. The spider walks around laying a non-sticky spiral. It returns to the hub, laying a sticky, insect-catching spiral and rolling up the first one.

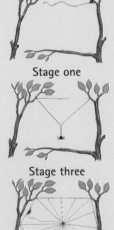

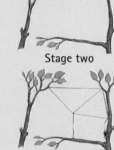

Stage one   Stage two

Stage three   Stage four

Stage five   Stage six

STRANGE BUT TRUE

The Little Miss Muffet of the nursery rhyme was based on a real girl whose father loved spiders. He believed that eating spiders could cure various illnesses, so he fed spiders to his daughter when she was sick. No wonder a spider beside her frightened Miss Muffet away!

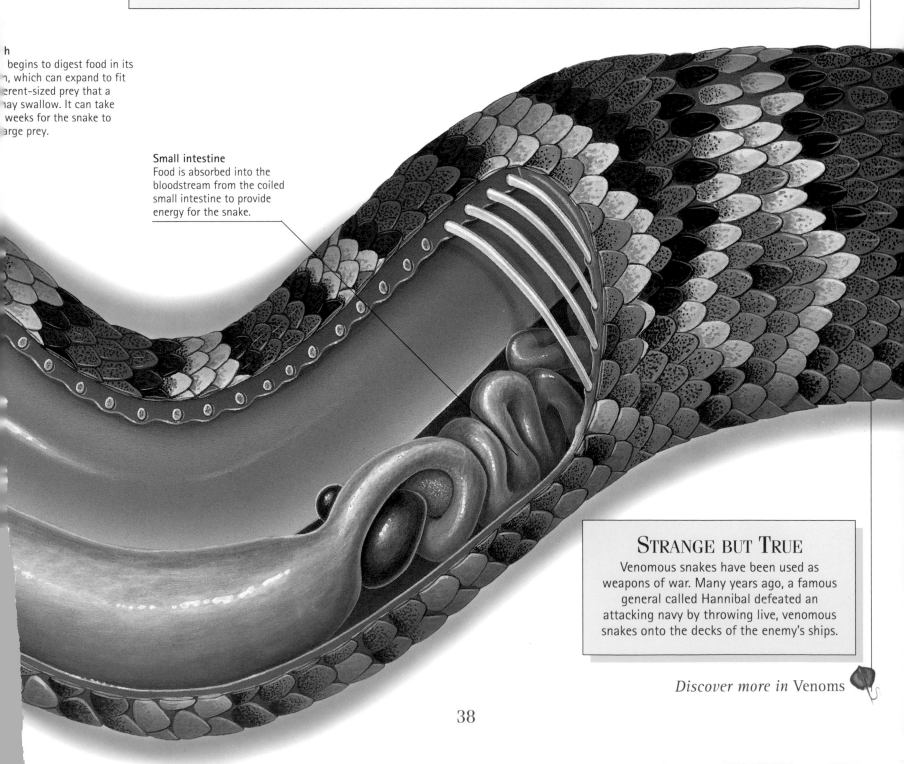

RATTLING AROUND

There are about 30 kinds of rattlesnake, and these are found only in North and Central America. The eastern and western diamondback rattlesnakes are the largest and most dangerous of them all. Rattlesnakes are famous around the world for their unique rattling tails. The tail has a series of interlocking shells or rings made of hardened skin. When a rattlesnake moves its tail rapidly, the rings hit against each other and make a buzzing, rattling sound. Some scientists think the snake rattles its tail to warn off large animals, such as people and cows, so it does not have to waste its venom killing prey that is too big to swallow. Other scientists believe the rattle distracts prey; they watch the snake's tail, and ignore its deadly fangs— until it is too late.

Western diamondback rattlesnake

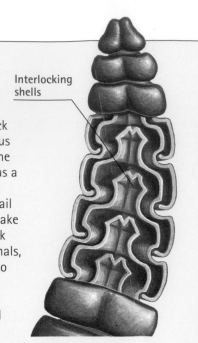

Interlocking shells

h

begins to digest food in its
, which can expand to fit
erent-sized prey that a
ay swallow. It can take
weeks for the snake to
arge prey.

Small intestine
Food is absorbed into the bloodstream from the coiled small intestine to provide energy for the snake.

STRANGE BUT TRUE
Venomous snakes have been used as weapons of war. Many years ago, a famous general called Hannibal defeated an attacking navy by throwing live, venomous snakes onto the decks of the enemy's ships.

Discover more in Venoms

38

Anaconda
33 ft (10 m)

Boa constrictor
14¹/₂ ft (4.5 m)

Eastern diamondback
rattlesnake 7 ft (2.2 m)

Yellow-bellied sea snake
2¹/₂ ft (0.8 m)

BIGGER IS NOT ALWAYS BETTER

All snakes have a tube-like body, but they vary greatly in size and length. The biggest snakes are not always the most dangerous. The anaconda is enormous and can squeeze large animals in its coils, but the small yellow-bellied sea snake has extremely potent venom. It can kill prey much larger than itself within minutes.

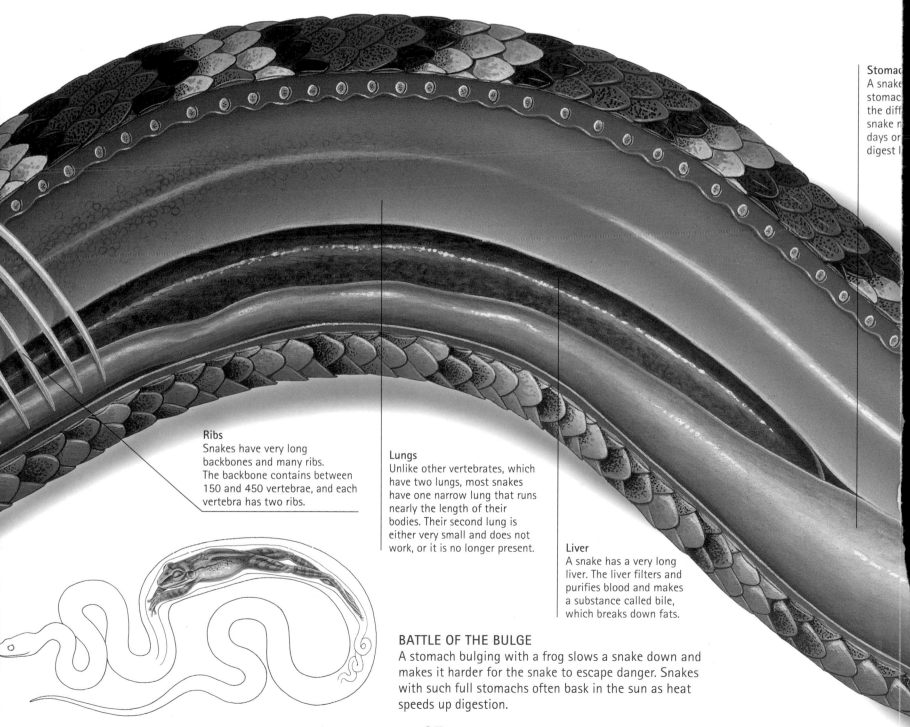

Stomach
A snake
stomach
the diff
snake n
days or
digest l

Ribs
Snakes have very long backbones and many ribs. The backbone contains between 150 and 450 vertebrae, and each vertebra has two ribs.

Lungs
Unlike other vertebrates, which have two lungs, most snakes have one narrow lung that runs nearly the length of their bodies. Their second lung is either very small and does not work, or it is no longer present.

Liver
A snake has a very long liver. The liver filters and purifies blood and makes a substance called bile, which breaks down fats.

BATTLE OF THE BULGE

A stomach bulging with a frog slows a snake down and makes it harder for the snake to escape danger. Snakes with such full stomachs often bask in the sun as heat speeds up digestion.

37

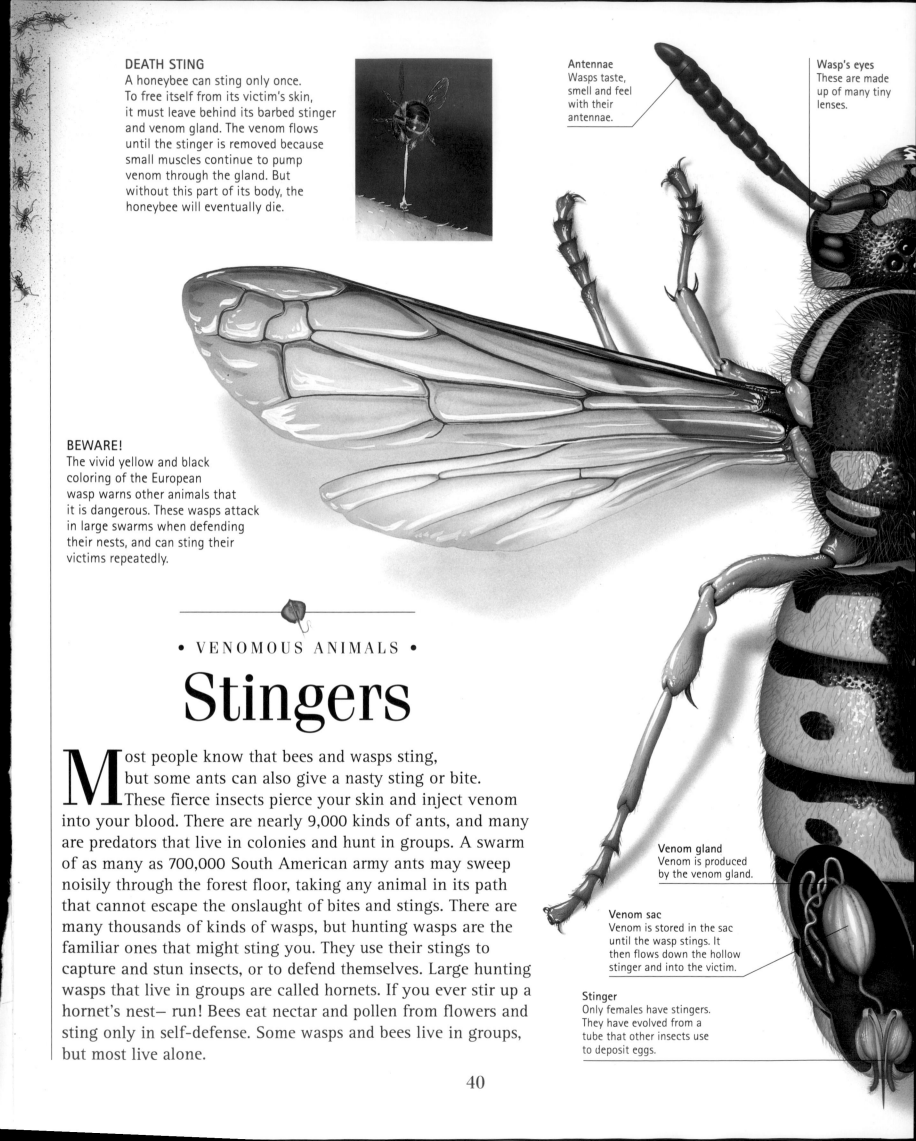

DEATH STING
A honeybee can sting only once. To free itself from its victim's skin, it must leave behind its barbed stinger and venom gland. The venom flows until the stinger is removed because small muscles continue to pump venom through the gland. But without this part of its body, the honeybee will eventually die.

Antennae
Wasps taste, smell and feel with their antennae.

Wasp's eyes
These are made up of many tiny lenses.

BEWARE!
The vivid yellow and black coloring of the European wasp warns other animals that it is dangerous. These wasps attack in large swarms when defending their nests, and can sting their victims repeatedly.

• VENOMOUS ANIMALS •

Stingers

Most people know that bees and wasps sting, but some ants can also give a nasty sting or bite. These fierce insects pierce your skin and inject venom into your blood. There are nearly 9,000 kinds of ants, and many are predators that live in colonies and hunt in groups. A swarm of as many as 700,000 South American army ants may sweep noisily through the forest floor, taking any animal in its path that cannot escape the onslaught of bites and stings. There are many thousands of kinds of wasps, but hunting wasps are the familiar ones that might sting you. They use their stings to capture and stun insects, or to defend themselves. Large hunting wasps that live in groups are called hornets. If you ever stir up a hornet's nest— run! Bees eat nectar and pollen from flowers and sting only in self-defense. Some wasps and bees live in groups, but most live alone.

Venom gland
Venom is produced by the venom gland.

Venom sac
Venom is stored in the sac until the wasp stings. It then flows down the hollow stinger and into the victim.

Stinger
Only females have stingers. They have evolved from a tube that other insects use to deposit eggs.

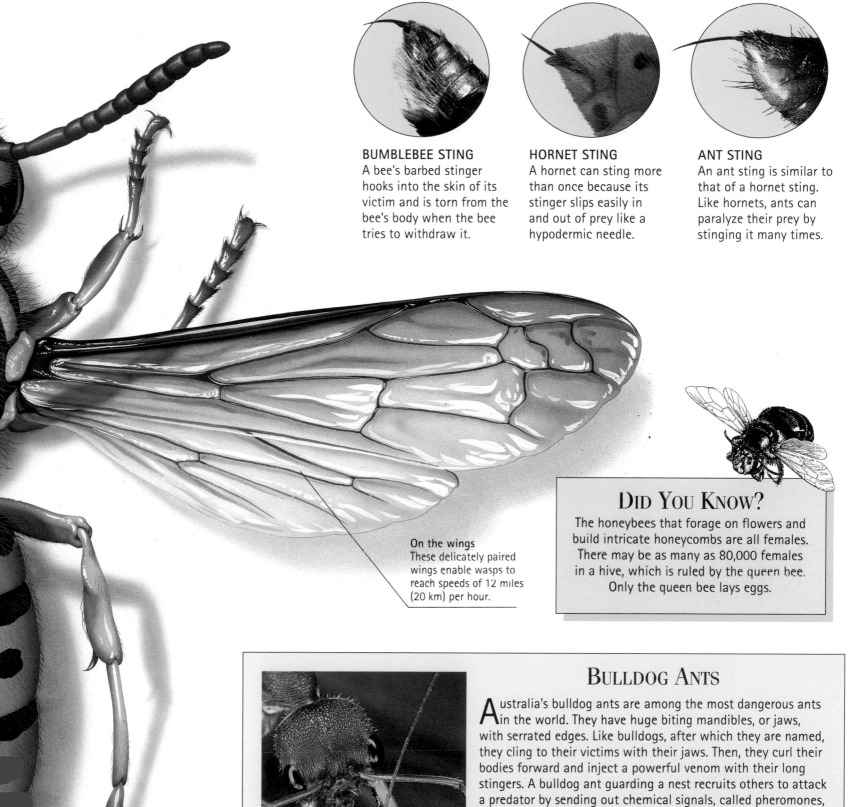

BUMBLEBEE STING
A bee's barbed stinger hooks into the skin of its victim and is torn from the bee's body when the bee tries to withdraw it.

HORNET STING
A hornet can sting more than once because its stinger slips easily in and out of prey like a hypodermic needle.

ANT STING
An ant sting is similar to that of a hornet sting. Like hornets, ants can paralyze their prey by stinging it many times.

On the wings
These delicately paired wings enable wasps to reach speeds of 12 miles (20 km) per hour.

DID YOU KNOW?
The honeybees that forage on flowers and build intricate honeycombs are all females. There may be as many as 80,000 females in a hive, which is ruled by the queen bee. Only the queen bee lays eggs.

BULLDOG ANTS

Australia's bulldog ants are among the most dangerous ants in the world. They have huge biting mandibles, or jaws, with serrated edges. Like bulldogs, after which they are named, they cling to their victims with their jaws. Then, they curl their bodies forward and inject a powerful venom with their long stingers. A bulldog ant guarding a nest recruits others to attack a predator by sending out chemical signals, called pheromones, which are produced in the Dufor's gland. As few as 30 stings from these aggressive ants can kill a human.

Venom duct

Dufor's gland

Stinger

41

Scorpios

HANDY LEGS
Like their relatives the spiders, scorpions have eight legs. Two of them have evolved into large pedipalps, which end in grasping pincers. Male and female sometimes join pincers and perform a dance during mating.

There are nearly 9,000 kinds of scorpions, none of them longer than your hand. A few, such as the Trinidad scorpion and the African gold scorpion, have stings that can be deadly, especially to small children. A scorpion usually lashes out with its stinging tail when a bare-footed person steps on it. But slipping into your shoes may be equally dangerous. Scorpions often seek warm, dark places— such as shoes— to sleep! Most scorpions, however, are harmless. They sting to defend themselves and to kill prey such as spiders, insects and small vertebrates. Their lobster-like pinching legs help them capture and crush prey.

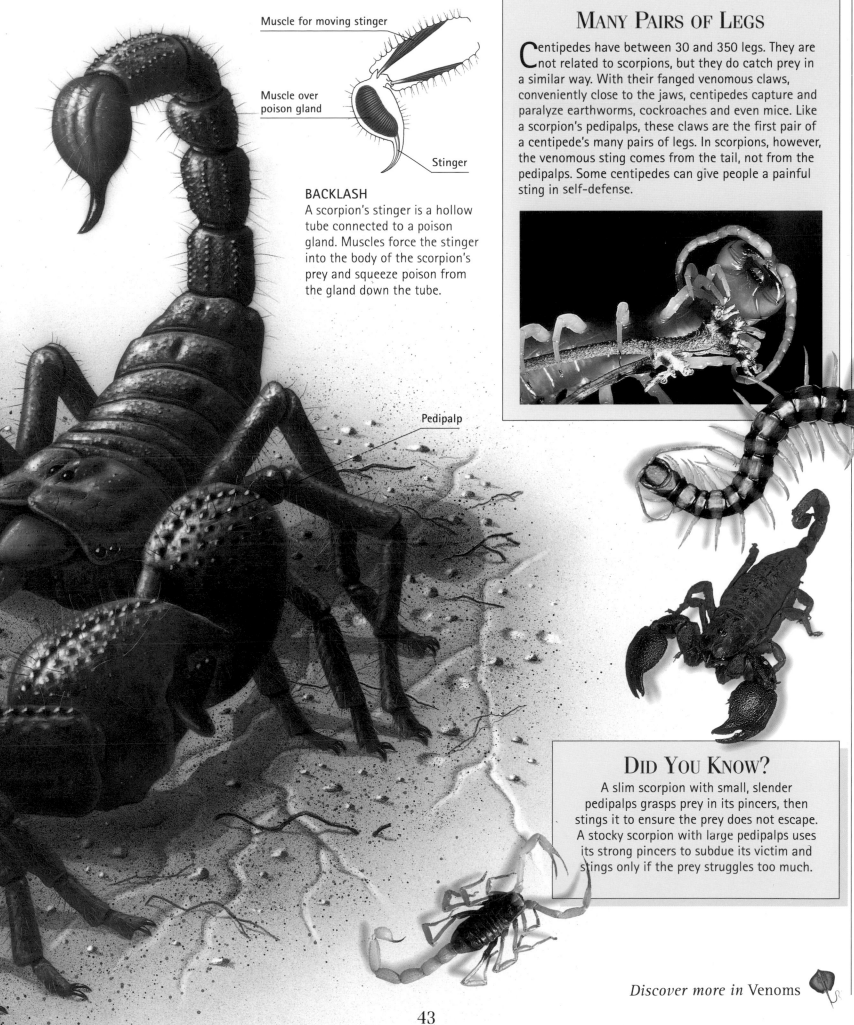

Muscle for moving stinger

Muscle over poison gland

Stinger

BACKLASH
A scorpion's stinger is a hollow tube connected to a poison gland. Muscles force the stinger into the body of the scorpion's prey and squeeze poison from the gland down the tube.

Pedipalp

MANY PAIRS OF LEGS

Centipedes have between 30 and 350 legs. They are not related to scorpions, but they do catch prey in a similar way. With their fanged venomous claws, conveniently close to the jaws, centipedes capture and paralyze earthworms, cockroaches and even mice. Like a scorpion's pedipalps, these claws are the first pair of a centipede's many pairs of legs. In scorpions, however, the venomous sting comes from the tail, not from the pedipalps. Some centipedes can give people a painful sting in self-defense.

DID YOU KNOW?

A slim scorpion with small, slender pedipalps grasps prey in its pincers, then stings it to ensure the prey does not escape. A stocky scorpion with large pedipalps uses its strong pincers to subdue its victim and stings only if the prey struggles too much.

Discover more in Venoms

43

Fish

It may seem surprising, but fish can kill people. Some fish can cause very painful injuries or even death by injecting venom into a victim's flesh with their sharp spines. Some fish have as many as 18 spines on their backs, while others have spines at the ends of their tails. Venomous fish live in oceans around the world. A few, such as catfish, live in rivers. In most fish, venomous spines are a defense against predators. In shallow coastal waters, people can come into contact with venomous fish, such as weevers and stonefish, which lie hidden on the ocean floor. A wader who steps on one is stabbed by the spines. Other venomous fish, such as lionfish and zebrafish, are beautiful and easy to see. People are stung when they touch them.

DANGER BELOW
The lionfish swims slowly and gracefully among the crevices of a coral reef. Its long, lacy and brilliantly colored fins conceal 18 needle-sharp spines full of deadly venom. The spines of a stonefish, lying motionless in the sand, are also venomous. An unsuspecting wader could easily stand on this well-camouflaged fish, which is covered with algae that live on its skin.

SURGEONS' KNIVES

Surgeonfish have thin, flat bodies. With incisorlike teeth, they nibble on small animals and plants living and growing on rocks or coral. These brightly colored, or dull, fish range in size from 8-40 inches (20 to 100 cm). On each side of their tails, surgeonfish carry sharp, venomous spines that flick out like knives when the fish are excited. Surgeonfish swimming in large schools may slash the legs of a wader with these spines, causing deep, painful gashes that are slow to heal.

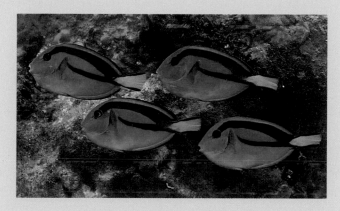

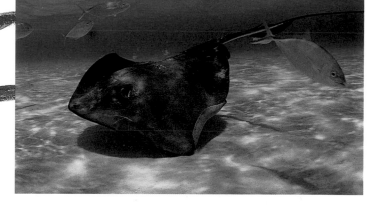

FLICK OF THE TAIL

Many stingrays live in warm, coastal waters, where they spend much time resting camouflaged on the sandy ocean floor. When someone steps on a stingray's back, it lashes out with its whiplike tail, which has one or more barbed, venom-filled spines. In the largest stingrays, the spines reach up to 1 ft (30 cm) long, but even the smaller stingray spines can inflict terrible, sometimes deadly, wounds.

Discover more in Venoms

45

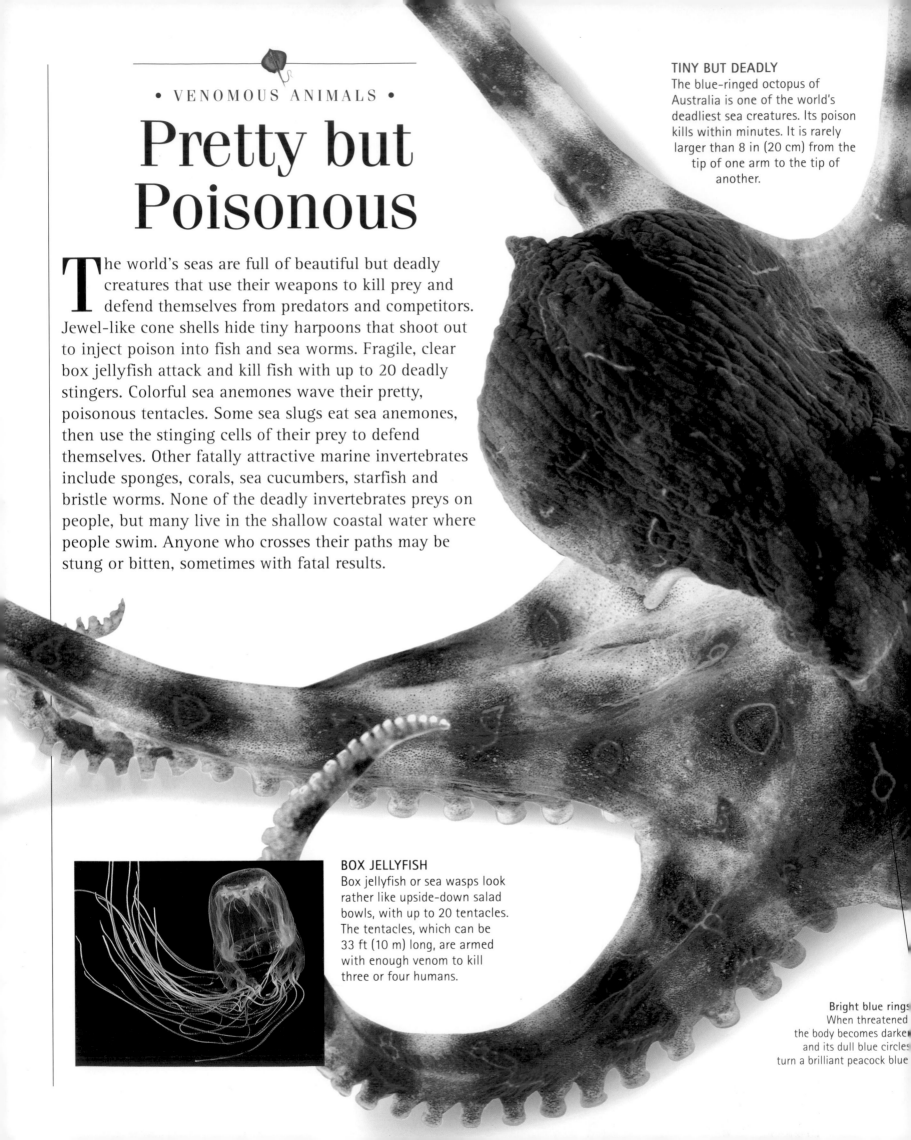

Pretty but Poisonous

The world's seas are full of beautiful but deadly creatures that use their weapons to kill prey and defend themselves from predators and competitors. Jewel-like cone shells hide tiny harpoons that shoot out to inject poison into fish and sea worms. Fragile, clear box jellyfish attack and kill fish with up to 20 deadly stingers. Colorful sea anemones wave their pretty, poisonous tentacles. Some sea slugs eat sea anemones, then use the stinging cells of their prey to defend themselves. Other fatally attractive marine invertebrates include sponges, corals, sea cucumbers, starfish and bristle worms. None of the deadly invertebrates preys on people, but many live in the shallow coastal water where people swim. Anyone who crosses their paths may be stung or bitten, sometimes with fatal results.

TINY BUT DEADLY
The blue-ringed octopus of Australia is one of the world's deadliest sea creatures. Its poison kills within minutes. It is rarely larger than 8 in (20 cm) from the tip of one arm to the tip of another.

BOX JELLYFISH
Box jellyfish or sea wasps look rather like upside-down salad bowls, with up to 20 tentacles. The tentacles, which can be 33 ft (10 m) long, are armed with enough venom to kill three or four humans.

Bright blue rings
When threatened the body becomes darker and its dull blue circles turn a brilliant peacock blue

MAN O' WAR

A Portuguese man o' war is a colony of animals living together. The gas-filled float, or bladder, is one animal, and the stinging tentacles clinging to it are other animals. Their sting may cause sharp pain, headaches and chills.

STINGING TENTACLES

Each tentacle of the Portuguese man o' war has black "spring-loaded" stinging cells, which deliver the venom.

POISONOUS CONES

Within their brightly colored and patterned shells, cones hide a secret and deadly weapon. If they sense prey, they extend a sensitive tube, armed with a tiny, barbed harpoon. The harpoon injects a paralyzing poison into the unsuspecting victim. Three species, including the tulip cone, have been known to kill humans.

Tulip cone

Aulicus cone

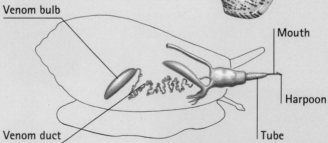

Venom bulb

Mouth

Harpoon

Venom duct

Tube

DID YOU KNOW?

The venomous sting of a matamala, a sea anemone from the South Pacific, affects people only mildly. Eating this creature, however, can be deadly.

Tentacles
Octopuses can move their tentacles at lightning speed to catch prey.

47

Hooves and Spurs

Every karate expert knows that a foot powered by a strong leg can deliver a stunning blow. It is not surprising that some animals have evolved kicking legs and feet as weapons. An ostrich, for example, usually runs away from danger. But a cornered ostrich is capable of killing with a kick. Other animals increase the effect of their kicks with additional structures. The toes of horses, deer and similar animals are encased in thick, sharp-edged hooves. Male jungle fowl have razor-sharp spurs, and the toes of cassowaries are like daggers. Animals use kicking mainly to defend themselves against predators. In some species, males kick in battles over females. Horses sometimes kick people who ignore the rule about never standing behind one.

FLYING HOOVES
To defend themselves and other members of their group, zebras kick predators such as African hunting dogs with one or both of their powerful back legs. When hoof meets head, the predator may be stunned, or killed. The hoof's sharp edge may also leave predators with bloody gashes.

HOOVED COMBAT
Even reindeer with antlers use sharp front hooves in fights over food. Rising on their hind legs, reindeer flail at each other with their front legs. In combat, the reindeer smacks a front foot into its opponent's body or slashes it with a sharp hoof.

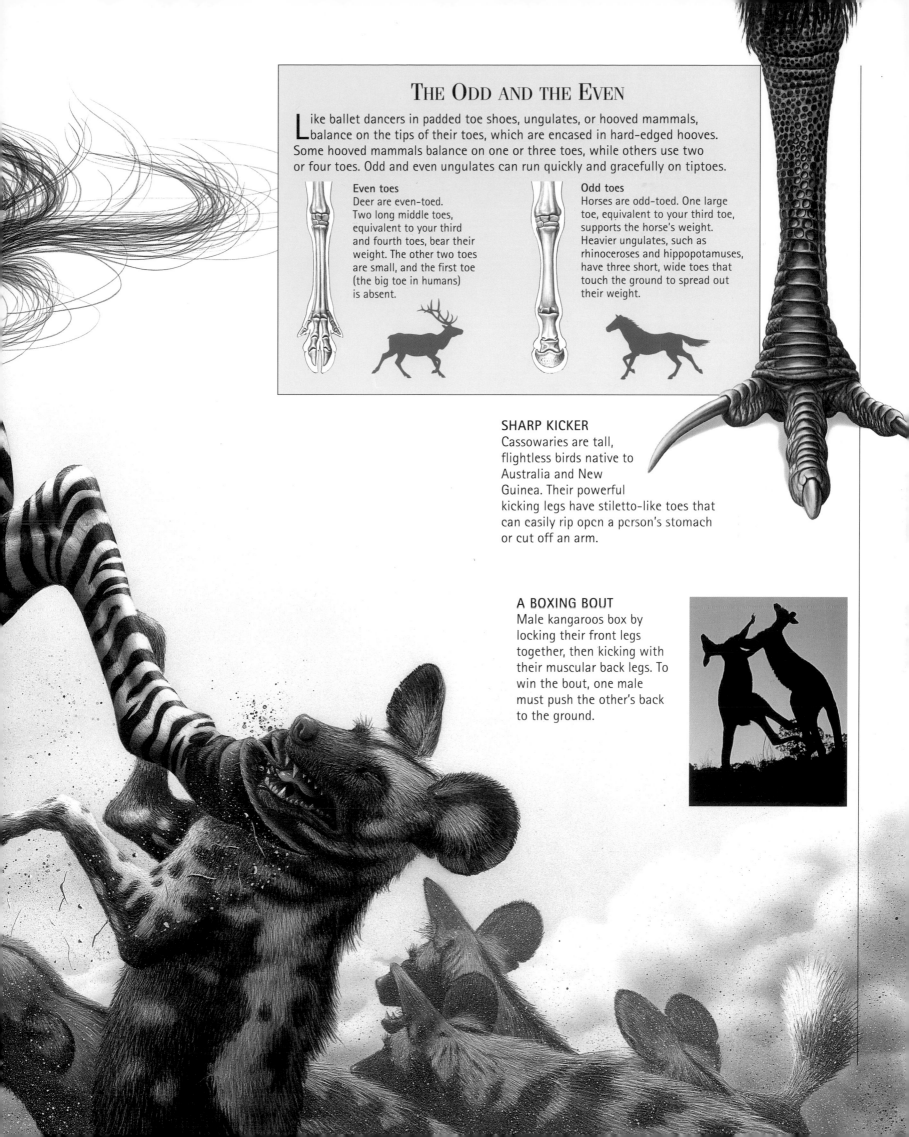

THE ODD AND THE EVEN

Like ballet dancers in padded toe shoes, ungulates, or hooved mammals, balance on the tips of their toes, which are encased in hard-edged hooves. Some hooved mammals balance on one or three toes, while others use two or four toes. Odd and even ungulates can run quickly and gracefully on tiptoes.

Even toes
Deer are even-toed. Two long middle toes, equivalent to your third and fourth toes, bear their weight. The other two toes are small, and the first toe (the big toe in humans) is absent.

Odd toes
Horses are odd-toed. One large toe, equivalent to your third toe, supports the horse's weight. Heavier ungulates, such as rhinoceroses and hippopotamuses, have three short, wide toes that touch the ground to spread out their weight.

SHARP KICKER
Cassowaries are tall, flightless birds native to Australia and New Guinea. Their powerful kicking legs have stiletto-like toes that can easily rip open a person's stomach or cut off an arm.

A BOXING BOUT
Male kangaroos box by locking their front legs together, then kicking with their muscular back legs. To win the bout, one male must push the other's back to the ground.

POISON FEATHERS
In 1991, scientists discovered that the skin and feathers of New Guinea's pitohui contain a poison similar to that of dart-poison frogs. Pitohuis are the first birds found to be poisonous.

• NATURAL WEAPONS •

Skin, Quills and Feathers

Beware of animals bearing bright colors! Very often, animals with vivid coloring have dangerous chemical defenses. Predators can easily see these creatures, but learn quickly to avoid them, or die. Many caterpillars and butterflies store toxins in their bodies; some cause a rash in people who touch them. The skin of some brightly colored frogs and other amphibians secretes poisons that range from mild to murderous. Some fish also have poisonous skin or flesh. Although scientists do not really know if this discourages natural fish predators, it certainly influences whether these fish appear on human menus! At least one species of bird has poisonous feathers, which, like hair, are a special form of skin. A few species of mammal have evolved different hairs called quills. Quills are not poisonous, but few predators are willing to risk a mouthful of needles.

SNEAKY SALAMANDER
The bright colors of the red salamander mimic those of the North American newt, whose poisonous skin and nasty taste repel birds and snakes. The red salamander is not poisonous, but many predators avoid it just in case.

BALL OF QUILLS

On hard ground, a threatened echidna curls into a tight ball of spiky quills, leaving no soft parts exposed to a predator's teeth. When the soil is soft, the echidna burrows into the ground until only its quills poke above the surface.

TOXIC TOAD

When they are frightened, cane toads, and many other toads, produce a frothy, white foam behind the eyes, which is a poison. The chemicals that make up the poison are strong enough to kill small animals.

A DEADLY MEAL

The skin, blood and internal organs of puffer fish contain a deadly poison. But in Japan, the flesh of the puffer fish, called fugu, is served as a gourmet meal. Fugu chefs are trained to keep the poison away from the flesh, but every year a few people die after a last supper of fugu.

FATAL FROGS

The Choco Indians of South America rub the darts for their blow guns across the backs of the bright yellow dart-poison frogs. Hunters then shoot prey, such as monkeys and tapirs, which die quickly before they can escape into the forest.

LARGE AND LETHAL
The Komodo dragon of Indonesia is the
biggest lizard in the world. With its strong
legs, fang-like teeth, lashing tail and
surprising agility, it can kill water buffalo
that are three times its weight.

• NATURAL WEAPONS •

Size, Strength and Speed

A house cat and a tiger capture and kill prey with similar weapons: sharp claws and long canine teeth. One sits in your lap, but the other is a dangerous animal. Size, strength and speed make all the difference with many animals that are dangerous to people. Anaconda boas, for example, can coil part of their long body around a victim and squeeze the life out of it. An elephant can simply crush a person. Right whales have rammed whaling ships or risen underneath and flipped them over. Most large dangerous animals, even lumbering hippopotamuses and bears, can run faster than humans over short distances. You could easily outrun a crocodile or a cobra, but they often strike so quickly that you would not have time to flee. In the animal world, danger really depends on your point of view: a cat purring happily in your lap is very dangerous to a mouse.

BLAST OFF!
A crocodile can leap straight up from the water to snatch a bird out of the air or grab a mammal on the riverbank.

DRAGON CLAWS
Komodo dragons use their strong toes armed with sharp claws to bring down large prey such as deer and wild pigs.

STRANGE BUT TRUE
The fire-breathing dragon is a symbol of the Chinese people, but no one really knows the origin of the dragon myth. The Komodo dragon is certainly a fierce creature, and some people believe that the myth of a monstrous dragon was based on a reptile such as a snake, alligator or lizard.

SURPRISE
A group of orcas, or killer whales, swims deliberately close to, and sometimes onto, the shore near unsuspecting seals.

ATTACK!
The seals panic and try to flee into the surf. Here, the orcas may "play" with the seals until they are too weak to escape.

FIRST PAST THE POST
Cheetahs are the fastest land mammals and can reach speeds of 68 miles (110 km) per hour in seconds. Wolves take off more slowly and at top speed can run at about 37 miles (60 km) per hour. But a wolf can overtake a cheetah, because cheetahs wear out quickly. Wolves are long-distance runners, and can keep going for much longer at their slower pace.

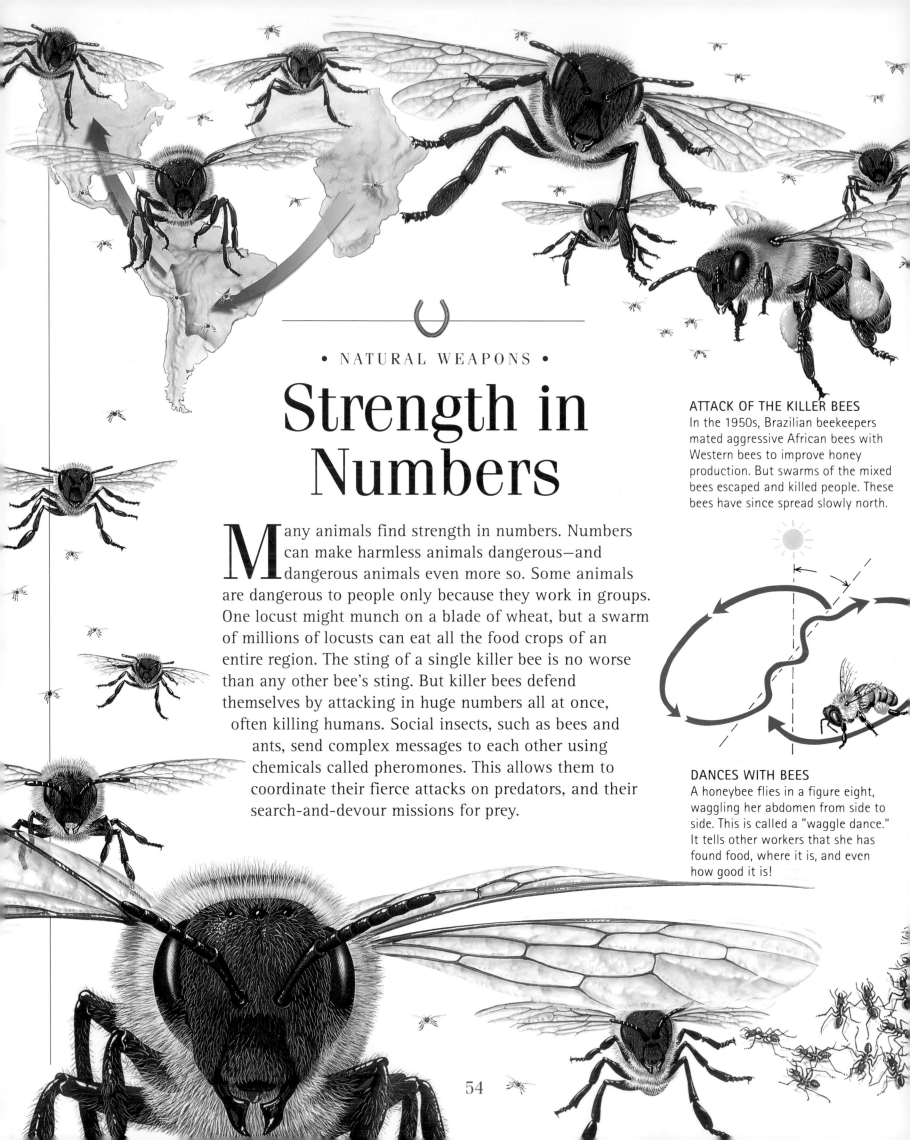

Strength in Numbers

Many animals find strength in numbers. Numbers can make harmless animals dangerous—and dangerous animals even more so. Some animals are dangerous to people only because they work in groups. One locust might munch on a blade of wheat, but a swarm of millions of locusts can eat all the food crops of an entire region. The sting of a single killer bee is no worse than any other bee's sting. But killer bees defend themselves by attacking in huge numbers all at once, often killing humans. Social insects, such as bees and ants, send complex messages to each other using chemicals called pheromones. This allows them to coordinate their fierce attacks on predators, and their search-and-devour missions for prey.

ATTACK OF THE KILLER BEES
In the 1950s, Brazilian beekeepers mated aggressive African bees with Western bees to improve honey production. But swarms of the mixed bees escaped and killed people. These bees have since spread slowly north.

DANCES WITH BEES
A honeybee flies in a figure eight, waggling her abdomen from side to side. This is called a "waggle dance." It tells other workers that she has found food, where it is, and even how good it is!

54

DEADLY DRIVERS

A raiding swarm of African driver ants kills everything in its path. Confined or injured animals cannot escape 20 million biting mouths. But the swarm travels slowly and humans have time to flee the ant onslaught.

NATURAL INSECTICIDES

The green weaver ants of Asia attack in great numbers, biting their victims ferociously with sharp, powerful jaws. They live in leaf nests and form huge colonies of up to half a million members. Weavers are excellent insect hunters. They forage in groups and work together to kill and carry back to the colony insects that are much bigger than themselves. For nearly 2,000 years, Chinese farmers have used green weaver ants to kill the insects that eat their crops.

A PLAGUE OF LOCUSTS

When the weather is warm, locusts form huge swarms and travel widely in search of green plant food. One of the biggest swarms ever seen in East Africa had 40,000 million locusts. They ate enough grain to feed one million people for a year.

Disease Carriers

Rats, blood-sucking mosquitoes, flies and ticks are the mass murderers of the animal world. Each year, dangerous animals such as big cats, crocodiles and cobras kill a few thousand people. But millions of people are killed or made sick by animals without sharp teeth, great size or venomous fangs. These animals carry a variety of microscopic creatures, such as bacteria and parasites, which cause disease and death. Some mosquitoes have a parasite called *Plasmodium*. When people are bitten by a mosquito with this parasite, they can develop malaria, a severe and often fatal disease. Scientists estimate that about half the people in the world, mostly in the tropics, either have malaria or are in danger of getting it. For more than a century, they have been struggling to eliminate the mosquitoes with various pesticides and to kill the parasite with different drugs. But again and again, these animals develop resistance to new types of chemical weapons.

A FEVERISH BITE
Some kinds of mosquitoes pass on the malaria parasite when they bite. Others, such as the one above, transmit the viruses that cause yellow fever and dengue fever.

Before

FULL TO BURSTING
After two days of sucking blood, a female tick blows up to 200 times its weight.

After

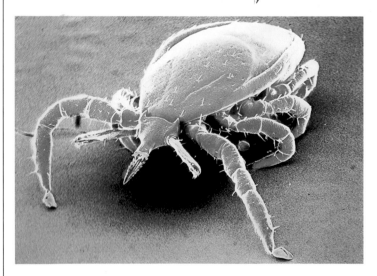

THE TICK OF LYME
Ticks live on blood from vertebrates, and many carry deadly diseases from one meal to the next. Deer ticks carry bacteria that causes Lyme disease, which can kill people.

BLACK DEATH

The deadly bubonic plague swept through Europe in the Middle Ages. Between 1346 and 1350, one-third of the population died from this disease, which was spread by fleas living on the black rat of Asia. Today, rats still spread diseases such as typhus.

THE MITES AMONG US

Did you know that eight-legged creatures, too small to see without a microscope, are feeding on your skin at this very moment? Dust mites are everywhere: in the curtains and carpet, in the furniture, in the wallpaper, and even on your mattress. They feed on the millions of dead skin and hair cells we shed continuously. Dust mites get rid of dust, but some people are allergic to them and can suffer from asthma.

THE LIFE OF A MOSQUITO

Mosquitoes lay their eggs in water. The eggs become larvae, which attach to the water's surface with a breathing siphon and feed on tiny plants and animals. Larvae turn into pupae, and then become adult mosquitoes.

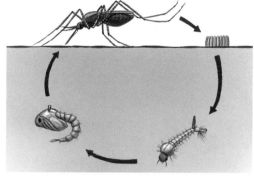

DEADLIER THAN THE MALE

Only female mosquitoes are able to suck blood. They need to have blood after mating so they can lay their eggs.

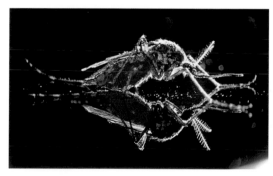

A REAL VAMPIRE

There are many chilling stories of vampires that suck human blood. It is true that the common vampire bat feeds on the blood of mammals. But does this include people? Very rarely.

Dangerous People

People are the most dangerous animals of all. They kill each other, and they threaten animals and environments everywhere. For thousands of years, people armed with weapons, from simple bone blades to modern submachine guns, have been killing other animals. The first North Americans wiped out mammoths and giant ground sloths. The Maoris in New Zealand destroyed moas and giant eagles completely. European explorers exterminated Steller's sea cows, elephant birds and other animals on islands around the world. Between 1970 and 1993, poachers in Africa slaughtered more than 60,000 black rhinoceroses. With fewer than 2,500 rhinoceroses left, this animal is now on the verge of extinction. Whenever people move into new habitats, other animals are moved out, by one means or another. This process continues as the growing human population, armed with modern weapons, invades the world's last wildernesses.

IVORY IN FLAMES
In 1989, Kenyan wildlife officials confiscated and burned the tusks of about 1,000 elephants to show their support for banning the ivory trade. Ivory prices, and the poaching of elephants, have now declined as a result of the ban.

SMART WEAPONS
People use their natural weapon, intelligence, to make tools that kill at a distance. Even simple bows and arrows allow people to kill the most dangerous prey with little risk to themselves.

THE SKIN TRADE
The beautiful fur of the spotted cat has tempted many hunters, and the numbers of some species have declined dramatically. In the 1970s, most countries agreed to stop the trade in skins of endangered cats.

EXTINCTION IN SIGHT

Rhinoceroses have been hunted for their horns for centuries. Horns are still prized ingredients in some medicines and are valued as status symbols when carved into dagger handles. Modern weapons and vehicles make it much easier to hunt these huge animals. Because of this, all five rhinoceros species may soon be extinct.

CARING FOR KOALAS

Koalas are not usually afraid of people. In the past they were an easy target for hunters who wanted their fur, and two million skins were exported from Australia in 1924. Soon after this, it became illegal to hunt these marsupials.

DID YOU KNOW?

In 1963, only about 400 breeding pairs of bald eagles were left in the United States. A 30-year effort to save them included protecting their habitat, banning the insecticide DDT and hunting. This was so successful that the number of breeding pairs grew to more than four thousand. The bald eagle is no longer an endangered species.

FROM THE OTHER SIDE

This protestor is part of a movement to save rainforests. Each year, people log or burn huge areas of rainforest, and more than 15,000 species of plants and animals become extinct. Unless this stops, all rainforests will be destroyed in the next 30 years.

FATAL FASHION

Crocodiles, alligators, snakes and lizards are killed regularly to make leather boots, belts and purses for the fashion industry. Many species of these reptiles are now endangered as a result.

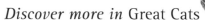

Discover more in Great Cats

— Where in the World? —

Dangerous animals are everywhere. Sharks and venomous jellyfish and reef fish haunt coasts around the world. Poisonous snakes and spiders live in every continent except Antarctica. Most continents have at least one predator– perhaps a crocodile, a bear or a great cat– that is larger than humans.

We are more likely to be struck by lightning than attacked by one of these dangerous animals. But there are many other dangerous animals we should worry about. Disease-carrying mosquitoes, houseflies and rats have invaded nearly every corner of the globe.

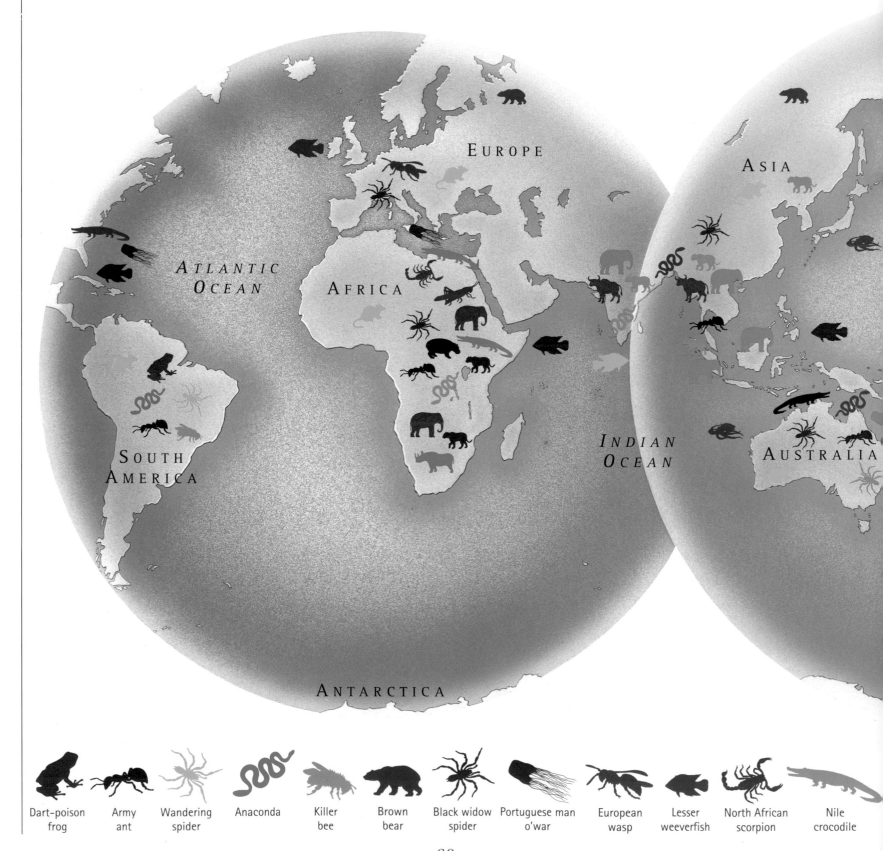

EUROPE

ASIA

ATLANTIC OCEAN

AFRICA

SOUTH AMERICA

INDIAN OCEAN

AUSTRALIA

ANTARCTICA

| Dart-poison frog | Army ant | Wandering spider | Anaconda | Killer bee | Brown bear | Black widow spider | Portuguese man o'war | European wasp | Lesser weeverfish | North African scorpion | Nile crocodile |

Tiger

 Asian elephant

 Gaur

Black rat

 Estuarine crocodile

King cobra

 Grizzly bear

Western diamond rattlesnake

American alligator

Barracuda

Scorpion

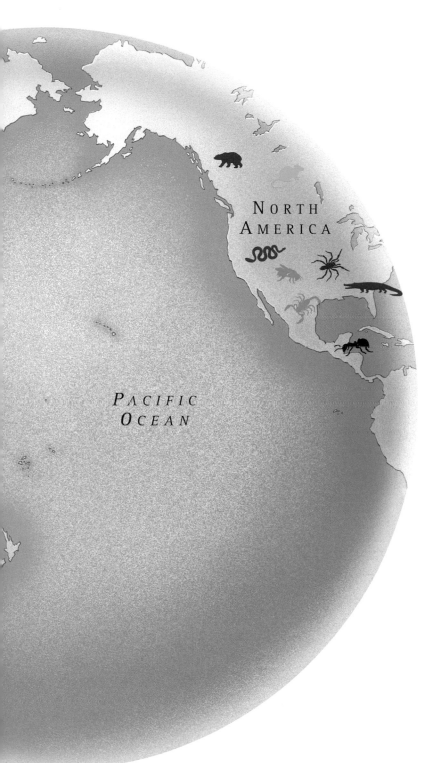

NORTH AMERICA

PACIFIC OCEAN

ANIMALS IN DANGER

People endanger animals. They destroy animals' habitats to build houses and towns, to grow timber, to graze other animals or to use as farmland. People also hunt different animals for their skins, fur or horns. If many animals of one species are killed, there are sometimes not enough left to breed. Two hundred years ago, one animal species died out each year. Today, several species become extinct every day.

POLAR BEAR
People in the Arctic have hunted polar bears for many centuries. In 1973, rules were set down to help control the number of bears being killed.

GORILLA
Gorillas were once hunted for their hands and feet, which were made into tourist souvenirs. It is now illegal to hunt gorillas, but some species remain dangerously close to extinction.

HARPY EAGLE
Harpy eagles live in the lush Amazon rainforest. But this powerful bird of prey is threatened as more and more of the rainforest is cleared.

CHEETAH
Cheetahs are the fastest animals on land, but they cannot escape the danger that faces their species. Much of their habitat has been turned into farms and many are shot when they attack farm animals.

 Hippo

 Desert locust

 White rhino

Spitting cobra

 African elephant

Lion

 Bulldog ant

 Black-headed sea snake

 Box jellyfish

 Funnel-web spider

 Stonefish

 Blue-ringed octopus

Glossary

abdomen In insects and spiders, the large area of the body behind the head and thorax that holds organs for digestion, excretion and reproduction.

amphibians Vertebrate animals that can live on land and in water. They include frogs, salamanders, toads and newts.

antennae A pair of sensitive feelers on an insect's head.

antivenin A medicine to counteract the effects of venom from snake bites and the bites or stings of other venomous animals.

antlers Bony growths from the head of deer and moose that grow and shed during the year. They are used as weapons and for display.

beak The sharp, sometimes hooked bill of a bird of prey, which is used to spear, carry and tear prey.

birds of prey Flesh-eating birds, such as hawks, eagles, owls and vultures.

camouflage The way an animal blends into its environment or looks like another animal in order to sneak up on prey or avoid enemies.

canine teeth The teeth between the front incisors and the side molars of mammals.

cephalothorax The six-part head and thorax of a spider.

chelicerae Pincerlike biting mouthparts found in spiders, scorpions, ticks and mites.

claws Sharp, curved nails on the toes of mammals that are used to catch prey, to dig and to climb.

colony A group of animals that live, hunt and defend themselves together.

competitors Two or more animals that may fight for the same food, territory or mating partner.

conservation Looking after the Earth's resources for future generations.

endangered species Animals that are likely to die out completely unless people take action to save them.

extinct No longer living. When the last living member of a species dies, the species is extinct.

fangs Long, hollow teeth in snakes and spiders that pierce flesh and inject venom.

fish A group of vertebrate animals adapted to living in water, with gills for breathing.

heat-sensitive pit Sense organs in some snakes that detect tiny changes in temperature.

hooves The toes of horses, deer, antelope and related animals that are covered in thick, hard skin with sharp edges.

horn An outgrowth on the head of rhinoceroses, antelope and wild cattle that is used for fighting and for defense. Rhino horns are made of skin; other horns are bone covered with skin, and are permanent.

insects A large group of small animals with three-part bodies, six legs, and usually two pairs of wings. It includes flies, mosquitoes, bees and ants.

invertebrates Animals without backbones, including insects, spiders, octopus, jellyfish, cones and many others.

ivory The hard white substance that forms the main part of an elephant's tusks.

mammals A group of vertebrates that feeds its young with milk. It includes cats, dogs, rats, monkeys, deer, whales and people, among other creatures.

mandibles The biting jaws of an insect.

mites Very tiny eight-legged invertebrate animals related to ticks. Many are parasites that can cause diseases in humans.

molars The side "cheek" teeth of a mammal.

paralyze To cause the loss of some or all parts of a body's ability to work, move and feel.

parasite An animal that lives and feeds on another animal, sometimes with harmful effects.

pedipalps A specialized appendage on the cephalothorax of spiders and scorpions used for reproduction by male spiders and as pincers in scorpions.

pheromones Chemicals produced by animals that send a message to others of the same species.

pincers The large claws of a scorpion's pedipalps.

plankton Tiny marine plants and animals.

poach To hunt animals illegally. A person who does this is called a poacher.

Black widow spider

Surgeonfish

Echidna

Crocodile

Black rhino

poison A substance that causes illness or death when touched or eaten, even in very small amounts.

pores Tiny openings in the skin.

predator An animal that hunts, kills and eats other animals (prey) to survive.

prey An animal that is hunted, killed and eaten by other animals (predators).

quills Long, sharp hairs found on porcupines, echidnas and a few other mammals.

rainforest A tropical forest that receives at least 100 in (250 cm) of rain each year and is home to a vast number of plant and animal species.

raptors Birds of prey, including hawks, eagles, owls and vultures, which eat flesh.

reptiles A group of vertebrates with dry, scaly skin including lizards, snakes, turtles, crocodiles and alligators.

retractile claws The claws of cats that are normally protected in sheaths but spring out when the cat needs them to capture prey.

rodents A large group of mostly small mammals including rats, mice, squirrels, hamsters and guinea pigs.

sharks A group of vertebrate animals that live in water. The skeletons of sharks are made of cartilage while other fish skeletons are made of bone.

species A group of animals with very similar features. Members of a species are able to breed and produce young.

spiders A group of small invertebrate animals with eight legs. Some spiders make silk webs to catch prey; all use venom to paralyze prey.

spines Long sharp structures on fish that can pierce flesh and sometimes inject venom.

spinnerets The fingerlike appendages of spiders that are connected to silk glands. They have tiny spinning tubes at the ends through which silk flows.

spring ligament The tough tissue that controls the retractile claws of cats. When the ligament is stretched, the claws spring out of their sheaths.

spurs Sharp, clawlike structures on the legs of platypuses and some birds.

stingers Hollow structures on the tails and heads of insects and the tails of scorpions that pierce flesh and inject venom and saliva. Stingers of some insects also suck blood.

Saltwater crocodile

talons The long, curved nails on the feet of birds of prey.

temperate forests Forests growing in parts of the world, such as Europe and much of North America, where there are large seasonal differences in temperature.

tentacles Long, thin, moving structures on marine invertebrates that are used to feel, grasp and inject venom.

Salamander

ticks A group of small, blood-sucking invertebrate parasites with eight legs. They live on vertebrates and can transmit diseases to people.

tropical forests Forests growing in parts of the world, such as central Africa, northern South America and southeast Asia, with little differences in temperature.

Bear skull

tusks The very long teeth of elephants, warthogs, walruses and narwhals that are used in fights and in self-defense.

ungulates Large, plant-eating mammals with hooves. They include elephants, rhinoceroses, horses, deer, antelope and wild cattle.

venom Poison that is injected by animals into a predator or prey through fangs, stingers, spines or similar structures.

venom duct The hollow center of a snake fang through which venom flows.

venom gland The place in an animal's body where venom is made.

Lionfish

venom sac The place in an animal's body where venom is stored until it is needed.

vertebrates Animals with backbones. They include fish, amphibians, reptiles, birds and mammals.

waggle dance A display by bees to tell others in the hive where food can be found.

web A silk structure made by many spiders to catch prey.

Bear prints

Index

Picture Credits

(t=top, b=bottom, l=left, r=right, c=center, i=icon, F=front, C=cover, B=back, Bg=background)
Ad-Libitum, 23cr (S. Bowey). Auscape, 18cl, 48bl (Y. Arthus Bertrand), 46/47, 51tr, 62c (K. Atkinson), 53b, 53br (E. & P. Bauer), 24bl (N. Birks), 38tl, 61tl (J. Cancalosi), 61tr (T. De Roy), 39tr, 51bc, 51c, 59br (J.P. Ferrero), 12tr, 26br, 56/57c, 61bl (Ferrero-Labat), 16tl (J. Foott), 32bl (M.W. Gillam), 6b, 62tl (Y. Gillon/Jacana), 33tl (C.A. Henley), 52l (J.M. La Roque), 30bl (Mammi-France/Jacana), 53c, 53tr (D. Parer & E. Parer-Cook) 35b (J. Sauvanet), 32i, 32tl (M. Tinsley). Australian Museum, 15tl, 15tr, 17tr, 17cr, 17br, 25br, 50l, 63cr (C. Bento), 50tl (W. Peckover/National Photo Index), 4ti, 5ti, 6i, 30i, 32i, 34i, 35i, 40i, 42i, 43i, 44i, 45i, 46i, 58bl (H. Pinelli). Australian Picture Library, 29cr (G. Bell), 55r (J. Carnemolla), 12c (Corbis Bettman), 14tr (R. Grunzinski/Agence Vandystadt), 51bl (Orion Press), 58tc (T. Stoddart), 43tr (A. Tolhurst), 32r, 57r, 61br (Zefa). Esther Beaton, 5ci, 14tl, 19i, 27i, 48i, 50i, 52i, 54i, 58bc, 58tl, 59b, 59bl. Biofotos, 30tl (H. Angel). Bruce Coleman Ltd,16b (J. Burton), 50b, 63cr (J. Dermid), 11b (M.P. Kahl), 9b (E. Pott), 40t (F. Sauer), 43br

(A. Stillwell). Comstock, Inc, 19cr (G. Lepp). Mary Evans Picture Library, 9tl, 10cr, 10tr, 14c, 19tr, 20t, 24t, 28l. Michael and Patricia Fogden, 36tl, 36tr. The Image Bank, 23t (J. Van Os). Lansdowne Publishing, 29tr. Mantis Wildlife Films, 5bi, 11i, 30tr, 34tr, 55l, 56i, 58i (D. Clyne), 41tr (J. Frazier). Minden Pictures, 9tr (M. Hoshino), 26cr, 62bcl (F. Lanting). NHPA, 35tr (A. Bannister), 35br (G. Lacz). Oxford Scientific Films, 49r (J. Aldenhaven), 41tc (G.J. Bernard), 43b (S. Camazine), 63bcr (M. Gibbs), 56l (J.H. Robinson), 23bl (N. Rosing). The Photo Library, Sydney, 57tr (J. Burgess/SPL), 13 (Hulton-Deutsch). Photo Researchers, Inc, 45tr, 62tcl (A. Power). Planet Earth Pictures, 46bl (N. Coleman), 29t (R. Cook), 45br (G. Douwma), 14br, 41tl (G. du Feu), 24cl (N. Greaves), 4ci, 8i, 10i, 12i, 43r (K. Lucas), 6t, 41b (D.P. Maitland), 20bl (R. Mathews), 47t, 47tr (P. Scoones). Project Advertising, 30bc. Smithsonian Institution, NMNH, 14bl (C. Clark). Tom Stack & Associates, 56tr (D.M. Dennis), 30cl (D. Watts). Stock Photos, 59tr (L. Nelson). 56bl (Phototake).

Illustration Credits

Simone End, 33tr, 60b, 61t. Christer Eriksson, 6/7c, 12/13c, 14/15c, 16/17c, 18/19c, 20/21c, 24/25c, 28/29c, 42/43c, 48/49c, 58/59c. Wendy De Pauuw, 53c. Alan Ewart, 10/11c, 33c. Mike Gorman, 60/61c. David Kirshner, 2, 4l, 4/5b, 8/9c, 12bl, 16br, 18b, 20tl, 21r, 22/23c, 26/27c, 29tl, 30/31b, 31c, 33cl, 35–38c, 43tc, 47cr, 49tc, 50/51c, 52/53c, 57cr, 60/61c, 62bl, 63tr, 63br. Alex Lavroff, 28br. Kevin Stead, 1, 4/5t, 5tr, 5br, 34/39c, 40/41c, 41br, 54–55. Bernard Tate, 44/45c. Rod Westblade, endpapers.

Cover Credits

Auscape, FCtr (C.A. Henley), BCtl (J.P. Hervy/Jacana). Christer Eriksson, FC. The Image Bank, FCbr (J. Carmichael Jr.), Bg (R. Newman). Kevin Stead, BC.